VOLUME THREE
Small Group
RESOURCES

Other Student Impact Small Group Resources

Volume 1: Walking with Christ

Volume 2: Compassion for Lost People

Volume 4: A Lifelong Calling

STUDENT IMPACT

LEARNING

TO

SERVE

TWELVE

LESSONS

THAT WILL

BUILD THE

CHURCH

VOLUME THREE

Small Group

RESOURCES

BO BOSHERS
and Tricia Murphy

ZondervanPublishingHouse
Grand Rapids, Michigan

A Division of HarperCollinsPublishers

WILLOW
CREEK
RESOURCES

I would like to dedicate this curriculum to each of you with a shepherd's heart who has been called by God to serve high school students. I pray that the small groups on these pages will be a powerful resource for gathering students together and putting them on the path to becoming fully devoted followers of Christ. May God richly bless you for following the call He's placed on your heart to impact the lives of students … you are making a difference.

Serving together, one life at a time,
Bo

Learning to Serve
Copyright © 1997 by the Willow Creek Association

Requests for information should be addressed to:
ZondervanPublishingHouse
Grand Rapids, Michigan 49530

ISBN: 0–310–20127–6

Interior design by Jack Rogers

Printed in the United States of America

98 99 00 01 02 03 04 /❖ ML/ 10 9 8 7 6 5 4 3

CONTENTS

A C K N O W L E D G M E N T S

I would like to recognize and express my thanks to those who were instrumental in making this project happen.

To Tricia Murphy, who used her creativity, devotion, and desire to capture God's Truth for the result of moving students practically to find the love of Christ. Thank you for your friendship and sensitivity.

To Troy Murphy, my lifelong friend, who used his artistic gifts to help create the right format for sharing this resource. Thank you for your devotion to this project; I love running the race with you.

To Lynette Rubin, my friend and assistant, for her availability, support, and willingness to adjust when I needed it. I could not have done this without you.

To Dave Lambert, Rachel Boers, Jane Vogel, and their teams at Zondervan, who gave us understanding, support, patience, and direction in developing this project. Thank you for your time and energy.

And to the Willow Creek Association team, for the many people who were involved in making this desire for small group curriculum a reality. Thank you for the privilege of doing this project with you. Together we have seen a dream come true.

Introduction

You are holding in your hands an exciting tool! It's not every day that you can find a tool that will:
- assist you in touching the lives of high school students with whom you are involved—as a full-time, part-time, or volunteer youth leader;
- equip you to talk to your students in ways that will allow them to experience God in more intimate ways; and
- change the way you develop small groups in your student ministry.

Walk through the next few pages and catch the vision for this tool that will help you make a difference in the lives of high school students.

The next few pages are devoted to sharing a vision for small groups in student ministry. You will discover how small groups can most effectively be used to bring about life changes and specifically how to implement small groups using the experiences in this book. Take plenty of time to reflect on the impact these opportunities for community and growth can have on the students whose lives you influence.

WHY SMALL GROUPS?

Change—The Purpose of Small Groups

Small groups are essential to the development of spiritual life in those who want to be fully devoted followers of Christ. They are essential because community, growth, sharing, and discipleship happen in the context of a group. In Student Impact, the high school ministry of Willow Creek Community Church in Barrington, Illinois, we refer to our small groups as D-Teams (with the "D" representing the Greek word *Delta*, meaning "change.") Our mission is simply to turn irreligious high school students into fully devoted followers of Christ.

To accomplish this mission, Student Impact is based on a seven-step strategy. Everything we do fits into this strategy:

1. Integrity Friendship

   The process begins as we challenge our core students to build "relational bridges" with their non-Christian friends.

2. Verbal Witness

   After students have built credible friendships with their non-Christian friends, we teach them to look for opportunities to explain and discuss their relationship with Christ.

3. Supplemental Witness: Providing a Service for Seekers

   Student Impact, our service for seekers, is designed to nurture students' spiritual interest by introducing them to the message of Christ in a contemporary and relevant way. Impact is intended to be used as a tool by our core in reaching their non-Christian friends by supplementing their ongoing witness.

4. Spiritual Challenge

   At this stage of their friendship, we teach our core students to ask pointed questions that intentionally challenge their friends to consider the claims of Christ. We believe that once a seeker has spent time listening to God's Word and observing fully devoted Christian students, he will discover through the conviction of the Holy Spirit his need for a personal relationship with Jesus Christ.

5. Integration into the Body

Student Insight, our worship service for believers, is designed to mature the believer on the trek toward full devotion to Christ. Insight provides believers with an opportunity to participate in corporate worship and to listen to expository Bible teaching.

6. Discipleship Through Small Groups

Small groups provide a discipleship atmosphere. From this small group comes accountability, encouragement, and support, as well as Biblical teaching through learning experiences.

7. Ownership

At this stage of spiritual development, students are taking an active role in service within the church. Through both financial giving and using their spiritual gifts, they are owning their part of the Lord's work. A student now steps forward and takes the role of evangelist within his own circle of influence and thus begins a third spiritual generation. This occurs as he takes his non-Christian friends through the same seven steps that he traveled.

The vision of Student Impact is to create a unique community of students and leaders committed to letting God

- change their lives;
- change their friends' lives;
- build the church; and
- impact the world.

The four volumes of small group experiences, *Walking with Christ, Compassion for Lost People, Learning to Serve,* and *A Lifelong Calling,* are written with these four values (we call them "waves" of ministry) in mind. This book of experiences focuses on the third wave of life change: building the church. When a student takes ownership in his or her relationship with Christ and with friends, the next natural step is involvement in the church. This volume will assist you in sharing the vision for integration into the church body through tithing, using spiritual gifts, and being sold out for the cause of Christ.

For a fuller development of how small groups fit into the vision and mission of student ministry, see *Student Ministry for the 21st Century: Transforming Your Youth Group into a Vital Student Ministry* by Bo Boshers with Kim Anderson (Zondervan, 1997).

Authenticity—Leading by Example

As the leader of small group life, your role is not only to teach the Word of God but to be an example to your students. It's more than talking. It's living in the moment with students, thinking the way they think, asking questions that allow them to reflect on their world, creating an environment that provides opportunities for uninterrupted community and soul-searching. These moments are about helping students take the time to look at Christ and grow to be more like Him. It's about life change.

In Student Impact, D-Teams meet every other week. But our walk with Christ is lived out daily. Today's students are looking for leaders who live authentic lives in Christ. As a leader, you not only facilitate the D-Team experiences, but you work to help students view the world from God's perspective each day. The greatest lesson students learn is not from these materials but from your life. This can happen only through your commitment of time, prayer, and preparation. The D-Team experiences in this book will serve as the basis for group interaction, but the key to fully devoted followership is allowing God to work through you so that students experience Him.

If you're unfamiliar with the D-Team format, take a few minutes to read the following overview.

HOW TO USE THIS BOOK

For each small group meeting, you'll find Leader's Notes that will guide you through your preparation and actual leading of the group experience, and Student Notes that you can photocopy and distribute to your students to use during your time together. The Student Notes are perforated so that you can take them out of the book and photocopy the two pages back-to-back, then fold them to form a four-page booklet that your students can slip easily into their Bibles. (You'll notice that the page numbers in the Student Notes look out of order when they are unassembled.) Encourage your students to take their notes home, perhaps filing them in a notebook or binder, so they can look back at what they've learned throughout their small group experiences.

The Leader's Notes contain all the information in the Student Notes plus the following features to help you prepare and lead your students.

Unit Introduction

Each unit begins with an introduction that includes the Leader Focus and Big Picture. The Leader Focus will help you begin thinking about the unit theme from a new perspective. In the Big Picture, you'll find a brief description of the values and objectives for each unit as well as the D-Team experiences themselves. You'll also get your first look at the Unit Memory Verse. Each unit builds on the one before, but you can also use the units independently if that's more appropriate for your time frame or the needs of your particular students. You'll notice that the lessons within each unit are numbered independent of the other units to give you this flexibility.

Before the D-Team Experience

Each session has an easy-to-use summary outline that will help you see the D-Team experience at a glance.

• *Leader Devotion*—To impact students at the deepest level, there can be no mistaking the value of a leader's personal authenticity. The heart of the leader is key. This section will challenge you to recall personal experiences and gain new insights that you can share with your students. This mini-devotion will prepare you for the role of leadership.

• *Student Focus*—This section provides the leader with the rationale for the D-Team experience. It provides clarification on what a student can expect if he or she is committed to this experience and the truths to be learned. It may also provide an opening discussion question.

• *Unit Memory Verse*—Only four memory verses appear in each volume. When students focus on memorizing one verse per unit, they will truly have ownership of that verse and can apply it to their lives on a daily basis.

• *Practical Impact*—We believe students learn best when they experience God's truth, not just talk about it. Each Practical Impact section outlines ways for students not only to hear the Word of God, but to experience it.

• *Materials Needed*—Here you will find a list of everything you need to bring to the D-Team experience. Student Notes are provided for each D-Team experience and can be duplicated back-to-back for your D-Team members. Encourage your students to keep these notes in a binder so they can look back on what they've learned.

• *Special Preparation*—In this section, you will find detailed instructions to help you prepare for your D-Team experience. Phone contacts, letters, reproducible handouts, suggestions about advance phone contacts and letters, and other ideas for resources will help ensure that your D-Team experience goes smoothly.

• *Environment*—Because students are sometimes more able to freely experience God outside the context of four walls, each D-Team experience offers two options. Option 1 works in any setting, while Option 2 moves the experience outside a normal meeting room to an environment that has been created specially for the D-Team. Option 2 takes time and thought on the part of the leader, but it can set up a D-Team experience in a very powerful way. Explore your options. Figure out what freedom you have in this area. Depending on the size or structure of your student ministry, the environment can be established in different ways. If a large number of students meet together before they divide into different D-Teams, a master teacher approach can help to establish the environment by "painting a picture," then dismissing students.

Leading the D-Team Experience

Your entire D-Team experience should last approximately 60 minutes. It's divided into four sections: Get Started (5 minutes), The Experience (40 minutes), Reflection (5 minutes), and Make an Impact (10 minutes). Questions and Scriptures that are **bold-face and italic** in your Leader's Notes are duplicated in the Student Notes.

Get Started

During the first 5 minutes of the first D-Team experience of each unit, you will help your students: preview the objectives of the unit; understand the Unit Memory Verse; spend some time in prayer; and discover what to expect in this D-Team experience. In the next two D-Team experiences of each unit, you will use this time to review assignments and challenges from the previous D-Team experiences, encourage student-led prayer, and share objectives for the new D-Team experience.

The Experience

This 40-minute section is broken down into several steps to help you lead the experience. This is the practical work and discussion section for the students. You'll find step-by-step instructions along with discussion questions, Bible study, activities, and various practical exercises. Feel free to insert your own thoughts and insights—things God showed you during your Leader Devotion time as well as in your general preparation for the D-Team experience.

Reflection

This 5-minute portion of the experience will help your group members solidify the truths they have learned as they reflect individually on the experience. Encourage your D-Team members to truly invest in this section. Model for them the value of reflection as you work through the questions listed here. Don't be afraid of the silence of reflection as opportunities for growth are being formed in students' minds! Model openness in your own personal application, but especially encourage your D-Team members to share their ideas on how to apply the truths in their lives. Use the Summary Statements to reinforce the truths the students have learned.

Make an Impact

During the last 10 minutes of your D-Team experience, you have the opportunity to challenge your students to make personal applications of the principles they have experienced. Don't forget to seek God's guidance for each of your students.

• *... In Your Life*—Students like to be challenged. This section allows you to offer some sort of assignment and challenge to your D-Team members. Let them know they have a choice in accepting the challenges. Make it inviting to commit, but not easy. Remind your students that it takes training to develop godly character (1 Tim. 4:7b-8) that will bear fruit.

• *... With Accountability*—In this section, you will encourage each student to choose another person in the D-Team as an accountability partner. Together, they will work on the Unit Memory Verse. In addition, accountability partners will have opportunities to share their responses to assignments and challenges.

• *Prayer*—Be sure to close the D-Team experience in prayer. Model the value of prayer by upholding it before and after each D-Team experience. Invite your students to pray as they are comfortable. Explore this opportunity to pray in community with your D-Team members if you find that they are hesitant to pray aloud. You may ask certain students to pray for specific areas as you sense the development of community and safety.

FOLLOW UP

If you have more than one small group, you can use the Shepherding Summary Form (page 111) to enable communication between D-Team leaders and the ministry director. Duplicate this form and have each D-Team Leader in your student ministry fill it out after each D-Team experience. Simply indicate brief responses to the questions in each section. Over time, this process will assist you in accountability, opportunities for encouragement, record-keeping for D-Team member information, and direction-setting for your student ministry leader.

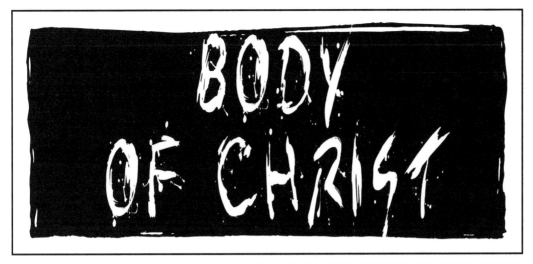

BODY OF CHRIST

LEADER FOCUS

Does the word *church* bring to mind a building? If so, you may have lost the true meaning of the word. The next time the phrase, "I'm going to church today," comes out of your mouth—stop! Evaluate what you've said. If the church is wherever God's people are, then wherever you are going that day becomes the church. You are asked to be the church in the world. We are honoring God not just while we worship in a building, but out there in the world.

BIG PICTURE

Unit Overview
In Unit 1 we will be focusing on the body of Christ by answering three questions: (1) What is the church? (2) Why do we need the church? (3) What part do I play in the church?

1. Body Parts
During this D-Team experience, your students will discover what God intends His church to be by answering two questions:

    Question #1: How did God design the church?
    Question #2: What should our response be to His design?

2. Growing Pains
During this D-Team experience, your students will discover why they need the church by identifying five spiritual growth needs that the church can satisfy:

    Need #1: Worship
    Need #2: Hearing the Word
    Need #3: Participation in the Lord's Supper
    Need #4: Fellowship
    Need #5: Vision and Mission

3. Body Language
Within this unit we have studied what the church is and how it can meet our needs. Now we will study what our approach should be as believers within the church. During this D-Team experience, your students will study two instructions Christ modeled for us while He was on earth:

Unit 1 Introduction

STUDENT IMPACT

Instruction #1: We are to come into the body of Christ with a servant attitude.
Instruction #2: We are to serve the body of Christ out of our love for Him.

Unit Memory Verse
"From him the whole body, joined and held together by every supporting ligament, grows and builds itself up in love, as each part does its work" (Eph. 4:16).

Unit 1 Introduction

Body Parts

Before the D-Team Experience

LEADER DEVOTION

When you hear the word *church*, what images come to mind? Your church building? People? Do you need a refreshing look at what God intended you to think of when you hear the word *church*?

Before you begin your study of the D-Team material, take a moment to get a fresh glimpse of the church as described in Ephesians 5:25–32. From these verses you can see that Christ's love for His church—you—is: unconditional, unbounded, unknowable, unmerited, undeserved, unequaled, and unparalleled. Take some silent moments to let that sink in before moving on. As you prepare to lead, jot down your personal experiences and insights in the "Prep Notes" column so you can share them with the students.

LOOKING AHEAD

Student Focus
Every D-Team member will discover what God intends His church to be by answering two questions:
Question #1: How did God design the church?
Question #2: What should our response be to His design?

Unit Memory Verse
"From him the whole body, joined and held together by every supporting ligament, grows and builds itself up in love, as each part does its work" (Eph. 4:16).

Practical Impact
You will be starting this D-Team experience with an exercise in which students play the roles of different body parts and experience their importance in completing a project. You will relate that exercise to the church as one body with many parts.

BE PREPARED

Materials Needed
- Bibles and pens
- Duplicated Student Notes
- Puzzle with approximately one hundred pieces
- Notecards for the body parts
- Table to put the puzzle on and one chair
- Masking tape (Option 1)

Special Preparation
- Contact your D-Team members in advance and remind them to bring their Bibles (if they have them).
- Write the following body parts and their instructions on notecards to hand out

to your students. Duplicate each in case you have more students than you anticipated.

Body Parts:
- **Eyes**: You are the only person who can look at the picture of the completed puzzle. Your job is to describe the puzzle picture to the **Ears**. You will sit with your back to the rest of the body parts.
- **Ears**: Your job is to listen to the **Eyes** and relay the puzzle description to the **Mouth**. You will walk back and forth from the **Eyes** to the **Mouth**.
- **Mouth**: Your job is to listen to the **Ears** and relay the message to the **Muscles**. You will walk back and forth from the **Ears** to the **Muscles**.
- **Muscles**: Your job is to take the message from the **Mouth** and deliver it to the **Hands**, who will put the puzzle pieces together. You cannot use your own hands.
- **Right Hand** and **Left Hand**: *(make separate cards for each)* Your job is to listen to the **Muscles** and put the pieces where the **Muscles** tells you. You cannot talk during the exercise.

Environment

To set up the environment for this D-Team experience, you can choose one of the following. Option 1 works in any setting; Option 2 moves the experience outside your normal setting.

Option 1: Using masking tape, make a large stick figure on the floor of your meeting room. Tape the index cards labeled with the different body parts (see Special Preparation) next to the appropriate area of the stick figure. Set up a table nearby.

Option 2: Go to a fast food restaurant and observe for a few minutes, identifying the different people and different jobs involved in getting an order placed, prepared, delivered, and paid for.

Leading the D-Team Experience

(60 min. total)

GET STARTED

(5 min.) 🕐

Unit Preview
Have a student read aloud the following information from the "Preview" in the Student Notes: *As you work together through Unit 1: Body of Christ, you will learn about the body of Christ by answering three questions:*
  1. *What is the church?*
  2. *Why do we need the church?*
  3. *What part do I play in the church?*

Unit Memory Verse
Read aloud Ephesians 4:16, "From him the whole body, joined and held together by every supporting ligament, grows and builds itself up in love, as each part does its work." Explain that, just as the parts of the body help one another in the growing process, the mutual gifts and ministries of God's people help each of us to grow in spiritual maturity.

Student Prayer
Ask one of your oldest or spiritually mature students to open this new unit with prayer.

Focus
Share with your D-Team members that this week every member will discover what God intends His church to be by answering two questions:

Question #1: How did God design the church?
Question #2: What should our response be to His design?

THE EXPERIENCE

(40 min.) 🕐

Introduce this unit with an exercise that will accentuate the importance of different body parts in completing a project.

If you marked out the stick figure described in Option 1, have each student pick up an index card and stand in that place. Explain to your students that they can only do what their notecards instruct them to do. Feel free to participate with your students, but only if you can do it without dominating or controlling what happens.

Give the picture of the completed puzzle to the Eyes and ask that student not to show it to the rest of the D-Team.

Then give your students these instructions:
  1. You have fifteen minutes to complete as much of the puzzle as you can.
  2. Communication must always follow a logical path—from Eyes to Ears to Mouth to Muscles to Hands and vice versa.
  3. Be patient and have lots of fun!

Observe how your students work together as a team. Notice the victories and frustrations they have with each other and on their own.

- -

After fifteen minutes, bring the students together and ask these questions to debrief the Body Parts exercise:

- What did you like about the exercise?
- What was frustrating?
- Did you like the body part that you were assigned? Why or why not?
- Would you have liked a different one? If so, which one?
- If you all had been Mouths, would you have gotten anything accomplished? How about Eyes? Ears? Muscles? Hands?
- What is the positive side to having all different parts instead of just one to complete a project?

Question #1: How did God design the church?
With the Body Parts exercise in mind, have your students take a look at one of the symbols in the Bible that gives them a picture of the church and what our response should be. Ask one of your students to **look up Romans 12:4-8** and read it aloud. Ask: **What symbolism is used to describe the church?**

Ask another student to **read aloud 1 Corinthians 12:12-27**. Ask: **How many parts make up the body? How do verses 19–20 support the idea of diversity? What significance does verse 27 have for you and your friends if you are Christians?** (Make sure your students understand they are just as much a part of the church as anyone else.)

Ask another student to **read aloud Ephesians 1:19-23**. Ask: **According to these verses, who is the head of the church?** (Jesus is the head of the church.)

Have your group look at **Ephesians 2:18, 22**. Ask: **How do we communicate with the head of the church?** (Through the Holy Spirit.)

Have your students **read 1 Corinthians 6:19**. Ask: **Where do we get in touch with the Holy Spirit? Do we have to be in the church building?** (Point out that the Holy Spirit is present in each believer.)

Question #2: What should our response be to God's design?
Have a student **read aloud Ephesians 4:1–4, 12, 15–16**. Ask your students to **list some of the behaviors that indicate a person is part of the body of Christ.**

- **vv. 1–2**—humility, gentleness, patience, and love
- **vv. 3–4**—keeps unity within the body
- **v. 12**—helps prepare people for works of service
- **vv. 15–16**—speaks the truth in love, grows spiritually, builds the church up in love

 (5 min.)

REFLECTION

Review with your students what they have learned about the church and what God's intentions were when He designed it. Point out that God also instructed us in how we should respond to what He has given us. Ask your students to take a moment to think about their previous beliefs regarding the design of the church and answer these questions:

- What do you think God meant when He referred to the church in the Bible?
- Has this experience changed any of your previous perceptions of church?
- Out of all the behaviors evidenced by believers, were there any that you are living out right now in obedience to God?
- What, if any, response were you challenged to pursue?

Give your students a few minutes to record honest responses to the following questions, found in their Student Notes: **What was most meaningful to you about our experience today? What does God want you to do in response?**

Ask a student to read aloud the Summary Statements in the Student Notes.

Summary Statements

We learned today that . . .
- The church is made up of many parts, but is one body.
- Christ is the head of the church.
- The Holy Spirit gives us access to Jesus.
- The Holy Spirit lives in all believers.

MAKE AN IMPACT

(10 min.)

. . . In Your Life
Point your students back to Question #2: "What should our response be to His (God's) design?" Encourage each student to choose one of the behaviors that indicate that a person is part of the body of Christ, and decide how to display it to others over the next week.

. . . With Accountability
Have the D-Team members form pairs to become accountability partners for the week and to work on the memory verse. Have each student begin learning the **Unit Memory Verse** by writing it out in the space provided in the Student Notes.

Prayer
Bring the students back together and close with prayer.

1. Body Parts

Begin learning your memory verse by writing it out in the space below.

MEMORY VERSE
Ephesians 4:16

Preview

As you work together through "Unit 1: Body of Christ," you will learn about the body of Christ by answering three questions:

1. What is the church?
2. Why do we need the church?
3. What part do I play in the church?

Unit Memory Verse

"From him the whole body, joined and held together by every supporting ligament, grows and builds itself up in love, as each part does its work" (Eph. 4:16).

Focus

You will discover what God intends His church to be by answering two questions.

THE EXPERIENCE

Question #1: How did God design the church?

Read Romans 12:4–8. What symbolism is used to describe the church?

Read 1 Corinthians 12:12–27. How many parts make up the body?

How do verses 19–20 support the idea of diversity?

What significance does verse 27 have for you and your friends if you are Christians?

Read Ephesians 1:19-23. According to these verses, who is the head of the church?

Read Ephesians 2:18, 22. How do we communicate with the head of the church?

Read 1 Corinthians 6:19. Where do we get in touch with the Holy Spirit?
Do we have to be in the church building?

Question #2: What should our response be to His design?
Read Ephesians 4:1–4, 12, 15–16. List some of the behaviors that indicate that a person is part of the body of Christ.

- vv. 1–2

- vv. 3–4

- v. 12

- vv. 15–16

REFLECTION

What was most meaningful to you about our experience today?

What does God want you to do in response?

Summary Statements

We learned today that . . .
- The church is made up of many parts, but is one body.
- Christ is the head of the church.
- The Holy Spirit gives us access to Jesus.
- The Holy Spirit lives in all believers.

MAKE AN IMPACT

. . . In Your Life
Look back at question #2: "What should our response be to God's design?" Choose one of the behaviors you listed that indicates that a person is part of the body of Christ. How can you display it to others over the next week?

. . . With Accountability
With your accountability partner, talk about your responses to the "Reflection" and "Make an Impact" questions. Exchange phone numbers. Call each other this week to hold each other accountable to making an impact in your life.

name	phone

Growing Pains

Before the D-Team Experience

2

LEADER DEVOTION

"The danger is not lest the soul should doubt whether there is any bread, but lest, by a lie, it should persuade itself that it is not hungry" (Simone Weil, *Waiting for God,* G.P. Putnam Company, 1951).

We know that the church is there if we want to participate—we don't have a difficult time seeing that perspective. But sometimes we convince ourselves that we don't need the church—that we can live without it. That choice is one that leaves us weak and vulnerable, eventually killing our spiritual walk.

Where is your hunger level? Are you feeding your faith regularly? Take some time to meditate and pray about your own need to grow spiritually and how you are meeting that need. As you prepare to lead, jot down your personal experiences and insights in the "Prep Notes" column so you can share them with your students.

LOOKING AHEAD

Student Focus
Every D-Team member will discover why he or she needs the church by identifying five spiritual growth needs that the church can satisfy:

Need #1: Worship
Need #2: Hearing the Word
Need #3: Participation in the Lord's Supper
Need #4: Fellowship
Need #5: Vision and Mission

Unit Memory Verse
"From him the whole body, joined and held together by every supporting ligament, grows and builds itself up in love, as each part does its work" (Eph. 4:16).

Practical Impact
During this D-Team experience, your students will get a chance to interview two guests who will give them perspectives on the church and how it can meet their needs. They will be able to evaluate and apply what they learned from these guests.

BE PREPARED

Materials Needed
- Bibles and pens
- Duplicated Student Notes
- A legal pad for each student
- Optional: lights, microphones, video camera

Special Preparation

- Write the following interview questions on each legal pad in advance.
    1. Who is your pastor?
    2. What do you do when someone is in trouble and needs help?
    3. What type of outreach does your church do?
    4. How do the people at your church learn about God?
    5. What do you believe about the Lord's Supper, or Communion?
    6. How do people meet and develop friendships at your church?
    7. When and why was your church established?
    8. Would you say that you have grown while participating at this church?
- Arrange to have two guests visit your group. Guest #1 should familiarize himself with the following Scripture passages regarding the church in Jerusalem and be prepared to role-play a believer in the early church. Guest #2 should be a Christian from your church. Provide both guests with the questions listed above in preparation for their press conference.

Scripture passages for the church of Jerusalem

1. Began at Pentecost (Acts 2:47).
2. Pastored by James (Acts 15:13).
3. Had all things in common and was in one accord (Acts 2:44–46; 4:32–35).
4. Spent a good deal of time in prayer (Acts 2:42; 3:1; 4:24; 12:5–17).
5. Witnessed at every opportunity (Acts 3:12; 4:5, 33; 5:42).
6. Grew constantly (Acts 2:47).
7. Practiced baptism and the Lord's Supper (Acts 2:41, 46).
8. Sent forth missionaries (Acts 8:5, 14; 11:22; 13:1–3; 15:22).
9. Preached the Word (Acts 2:16–36; 3:13-26; 5:42; 6:4; 7:1–53).

Environment

To set up the environment for this D-Team experience, you can choose one of the following. Option 1 works in any setting; Option 2 moves the experience outside your normal setting.

Option 1: Set up the room to simulate a press conference, with one head table, chairs in rows, proper lighting, and a microphone for each guest. You may want to videotape the press conference and distribute press passes to each of your students.

Option 2: Start in your normal meeting room. When you are ready for the press conference, take your students to a different part of the building that is set up for a press conference as described above, or arrange to do it at your pastor's home or in a public setting.

Leading the D-Team Experience
(60 min. total)

GET STARTED

(5 min.) 🕐

Review
Have a student read aloud the following question under "Review" in the Student Notes: *Last time you learned about God's intentions for the church and His instructions regarding how we should respond to what He has given us. Did you do anything differently as a result?* Invite each student to respond.

Student Prayer
Ask one of your younger students to pray today.

Focus
Share with your D-Team members that this week they will discover why they need the church by identifying five spiritual growth needs the church can satisfy:

> **Need #1: Worship**
> **Need #2: Hearing the Word**
> **Need #3: Participation in the Lord's Supper**
> **Need #4: Fellowship**
> **Need #5: Vision and Mission**

THE EXPERIENCE

(40 min.) 🕐

Explain to your D-Team members that, if they are Christians, then they need to continue to grow in Christ. Just as they don't have to live at home to be their parents' children, they don't have to go to church to be a child of God. But in both cases, living apart from a person results in a weak relationship with that parent (or Heavenly Parent). Today, your students will see the benefits of commitment to church.

Need #1: Worship
Ask three of your students to *look up Colossians 3:16b–17; 1 Timothy 2:1, 8; and Hebrews 13:15.* Ask: *What spiritual need is described in these verses?* (Worship) Emphasize the importance of corporate worship with other Christians.

Need #2: Hearing the Word
Ask a student to *read aloud Colossians 3:16 and Romans 10:17.* Ask: *What spiritual need is described in these verses?* (Hearing the Word) Point out to your students that they need to be fed on a regular basis so that they can move from baby food to adult food.

Need #3: Participation in the Lord's Supper
Ask a student to *read aloud 1 Corinthians 10:16–17; 11:26.* Ask: *What spiritual need is described in these verses?* Note that Paul clearly instructs us to take communion together because we are one body, and we need to remember what Christ did for us on the cross.

Need #4: Fellowship
Ask some students to look up these verses and read them aloud: *Acts 2:42; 1 Corinthians 1:9; Philippians 2:1–4; and 1 John 1:6–7.* Ask: *What spiritual need is described in these verses?* (Fellowship) Explain that we need fellowship with other

believers, with Christ, and with the Holy Spirit.

Need #5: Vision and Mission
Ask your students to **read Matthew 28:19–20; Romans 10:14–15; and 2 Corinthians 5:20.** Ask: **What spiritual need is described in these verses?** (Vision and Mission) and **What is God's plan for His church?** (to share the Gospel with every creature.) Ask your D-Team members how they will keep focused on that plan if they are not committed to the church—the body of believers—that is carrying out the plan according to Scripture.

Summarize that believers have five spiritual needs that can be met in the local church. Those needs are: worship, hearing the Word, participating in the Lord's Supper, fellowship, and vision and mission. To further focus on those needs, simulate an interview with a member of a local church from Paul's day and from a church that is from our modern day and age.

Press Conference
Conduct a press conference with your guests. Explain that Guest #1 represents a believer from the early church in Jerusalem and Guest #2 is a member of a local congregation. Both have come to answer the same questions listed below. This will give your students both a biblical and a modern church example that fulfills all the needs identified today. Instruct your students to play the part of reporters who want to know what is going on at the two churches.

Distribute the legal pads (with interview questions that you wrote out in advance) to your students and ask them to do a little investigative interviewing with the two church leaders.

Close by asking if there is anything not on the list that your students would like to ask—briefly! After the interview is completed, thank your guests and dismiss them.

 (5 min.)

REFLECTION

Come back together and give your students a few minutes to record honest responses to the following questions, found in their Student Notes:
- *Did anything in the press conference with the two church leaders surprise you about either of the churches? What was it and why did it surprise you?*
- *Did you see anything that would benefit you as a result of getting involved in the body of Christ?*
- *Is there a need that you feel is not being met in your life? If so, what?*
- *Could your church meet that need? How?*
- *What was most meaningful to you about our experience today?*
- *What does God want you to do in response?*

Ask a student to read aloud the Summary Statements in the Student Notes.

Summary Statements

We learned this week that . . .
- Every Christian has basic spiritual needs that need to be met.
- God designed the church to meet those needs.
- It is our responsibility to pursue our involvement in the local body of Christ.

MAKE AN IMPACT

. . . In Your Life

Challenge your students to pursue a part of their church to meet the need that is not being met right now in their life. Whether that is worship, communion, fellowship, or one of the other needs, encourage them to reflect on it further this next week and then make a commitment to act on it.

. . . With Accountability

Have the D-Team members form pairs to become accountability partners for the week and to work on the memory verse. Have each student write out the **Unit Memory Verse** and recite it to his or her partner.

Prayer

Bring the students back together and close with prayer.

2. Growing Pains

Review
Last time you learned about God's intentions for the church and His instructions regarding how we should respond to what He has given us. Did you do anything differently as a result?

Focus
Today you will discover why you need the church by identifying five spiritual growth needs the church can satisfy.

THE EXPERIENCE

If you are a Christian, then you need to continue to grow in Christ. Today, you will discover the benefits of commitment to the church. Hebrews 10:25 tells us "Let us not give up meeting together, as some are in the habit of doing, but let us encourage one another—and all the more as you see the Day approaching."

Need #1: Worship
Read Colossians 3:16b–17; 1 Timothy 2:1, 8; and Hebrews 13:15. What spiritual need is described in these verses?

Need #2: Hearing the Word
Read Colossians 3:16 and Romans 10:17. What spiritual need is described in these verses?

. . . With Accountability
With your accountability partner, talk about your responses to the "Reflection" and "Make an Impact" questions. Exchange phone numbers. Call each other this week to hold each other accountable to making an impact in your life.

name _____   phone _____

Review your memory verse by writing it out in the space below. Then recite it to your partner.

MEMORY VERSE
Ephesians 4:16

Need #3: Participation in the Lord's Supper
Read 1 Corinthians 10:16-17; 11:26. What spiritual need is described in these verses?

Need #4: Fellowship
Read Acts 2:42, 1 Corinthians 1:9, Philippians 2:1-4, and 1 John 1:6-7. What spiritual need is described in these verses?

Need #5: Vision and Mission
Read Matthew 28:19-20, Romans 10:14-15, and 2 Corinthians 5:20. What spiritual need is described in these verses?

What is God's plan for His church?

REFLECTION

Did anything in the press conference with the two church leaders surprise you about either of the churches? What was it and why did it surprise you?

Did you see anything that would benefit you as a result of getting involved in the body of Christ?

Is there a need that you feel is not being met in your life? If so, what?

Could your church meet that need? How?

What was most meaningful to you about our experience today?

What does God want you to do in response?

Summary Statements
We learned today that . . .
- Every Christian has basic spiritual needs that need to be met.
- God designed the church to meet those needs.
- It is our responsibility to pursue our involvement in the local body of Christ.

MAKE AN IMPACT

. . . In Your Life
What spiritual need is not being met in your life?

What can you do to get involved in church so that need can be met?

Body Language

Before the D-Team Experience

LEADER DEVOTION

"If you are going to live for the service of your fellowmen, you will certainly be pierced through with many sorrows, for you will meet with more base ingratitude from your fellowmen than you would from a dog. You will meet with unkindness and two-facedness, and if your motive is love for your fellowmen, you will be exhausted in the battle of life. But if the mainspring of your service is love for God, no ingratitude, no sin, no devil, no angel can hinder you from serving your fellowmen, no matter how they treat you. You can love your neighbor as yourself, not from pity, but from the true centering of yourself in God" (Oswald Chambers as quoted in *The Draper Book of Quotations for the Christian World,* Tyndale House, 558).

Mr. Chambers reflects what Christ displayed for us while He walked this earth. We can glean some life-changing truth from it. Before you study for this D-Team experience, spend some time meditating and journaling about how it affects you personally. As you prepare to lead, jot down your personal experiences and insights in the "Prep Notes" column so you can share them with your students.

LOOKING AHEAD

Student Focus
Within this unit we have studied what the church is and how it can meet our needs. Now we will study what our approach should be as believers within the church. This week, your students will be studying two instructions that Christ modeled for us while He was on earth:

Instruction #1: We are to come into the body of Christ with a servant attitude.
Instruction #2: We are to serve the body of Christ out of our love for Him.

Unit Memory Verse
"From him the whole body, joined and held together by every supporting ligament, grows and builds itself up in love, as each part does its work" (Eph. 4:16).

Practical Impact
During this D-Team experience, your students will be asked to respond spontaneously to a physical need within the body of Christ. They will be able to evaluate their motives and determine their response when put in a similar position in the future.

BE PREPARED

Materials Needed
- Bibles and pens
- Duplicated Student Notes
- Materials needed for your serving project

Special Preparation

Plan a service project that will take approximately fifteen minutes to complete. If it is possible to extend your meeting time, then complete a little bigger project. Project ideas include: cleaning a church basement; planning a church service or special event; helping your church secretary with a mailing; working with your church janitor; completing a project at someone's home such as weeding, cleaning windows, cleaning the garage, etc. You don't have to make the project fun and exciting for your students, but you don't want it to be the most horrible job they have ever done. Anticipate some resistance and some enthusiasm—and treat both responses the same.

Environment

To set up the environment for this D-Team experience, you can choose one of the following. Option 1 works in any setting; Option 2 moves the experience outside your normal setting.

Option 1: The environment will vary depending on the service project that you select for your students. You may want to display Scriptures and/or quotes about serving around your meeting room.

Option 2: Following your service project, find a quiet place such as a park or a forest preserve to finish the Bible study portion of the experience.

Leading the D-Team Experience

(60 min. total)

GET STARTED

(5 min.) 🕐

Review

Have a student read aloud the following question under "Review" in the Student Notes: *Last time, you were challenged to get involved in a part of your church to meet the need that is not being met right now in your life. How did you act on that challenge?* Ask students to share what they did in response to that challenge.

Student Prayer

Ask a student to pray before you leave to do your project.

Focus

Share with your D-Team members that this week they will be studying two instructions that Christ modeled for us while He was on earth:

Instruction #1: **We are to come into the body of Christ with a servant attitude.**

Instruction #2: **We are to serve the body of Christ out of our love for Him.**

THE EXPERIENCE

(40 min.) 🕐

Service Project

Introduce your chosen service project by explaining that you or another person/family needs help with a project.

When you have finished the project, thank the person who gave your D-Team the opportunity to serve. Then discuss the following questions:
- What did you expect to be doing when you came today?
- How did you feel when I told you what you would be doing? Were you disappointed? Surprised? Excited? Not sure what to expect?
- Why did you feel the way that you did?
- What if this person whom we served today had saved your life?
- In what ways would that have changed your feelings about helping him or her? What if a person who saved your life had asked you to help the person we served today?
- Would the source of the request have changed your attitude toward the project?

Instruction #1: We are to come into the body of Christ with a servant attitude.

Explain that Jesus is the model for our lives. Matthew 20:28 records that Jesus told His disciples that He did not come to be served, but to serve, and to give His life as a ransom for many. At the Last Supper, Jesus settled a dispute regarding which disciple was greatest by saying: "For who is greater, the one who is at the table or the one who serves? Is it not the one who is at the table? But I am among you as one who serves" (Luke 22:27). *Jesus is God of the universe and yet He came to serve not be served.*

Ask: *How was Jesus a servant while on this earth?* Supplement your students'

Prep Notes

ideas with these examples: He turned water into wine at a wedding when all available wine had been consumed; on His first encounter with the disciples, He helped them catch a boatload of fish; He healed the centurion's son; He fed huge crowds of people; He washed the disciples' feet; He healed the blind man; He healed lepers; He served the disciples the Last Supper.

Help your students see that Jesus' actions on this earth were acts of service. If for no other reason than to be like Him, we should be servants to those around us.

Instruction #2: We are to serve the body of Christ out of our love for Him.
Explain that *there is another reason to be a servant to fellow believers.* Have one of your students *read aloud John 21:15-17*. Ask: *What does this passage tell us about serving?* (If we love Jesus, we are commanded to feed His sheep—to be servants)

Share with your students that our love for Jesus is what will motivate us to be servants. If we are serving out of self-gratification and a need to get recognition, we will be disappointed and discouraged. But if we serve out of obedience and a love for Jesus and what He has done for us, then we won't be so concerned with recognition from others.

Some of your students may express that they don't feel motivated to be servants to those around them. Use the following excerpt to give your students a fresh look at what Jesus did for them on the Cross. This fictional story is told from the perspective of what an angel might have thought regarding the death of Jesus.

> He became one of you. . . . Not for a moment, but for a lifetime . . . and for eternity. God became man. . . .
> And just when we thought [God] could not surpass this greatest miracle with another, there came the greater one. . . .
> That little hill, where little men were permitted to do unspeakable things to [God's] Son. My comrades and I jammed against the portal, begging permission to break through and strike down the cowards, to unleash the relentless wrath of heaven's army. We longed to raise our swords as one, to destroy every atom of the dark world. . . .
> Here were these puny men obsessed with the offenses of others against them, while themselves committing the ultimate offense of the universe, driving nails through the flesh of God. . . . Any one of us could have struck them all down, and we yearned to do it. . . .
> But Michael [the head angel] would not permit us. . . . For [God] would not permit him.
> . . . . We writhed in agony. . . . And yet we grew to know—though not completely understand—that all this was necessary to meet the demands of [God's] justice and his love. He did not need us to rescue him. With a single word, with merely a thought, he could have unmade all men, destroyed the universe. . . . But he did not. He would not. He did not go there to be rescued. He went there to rescue.
> . . . . I will never understand it. . . .
> . . . . These . . . are things you will never fully understand either—yet I sense that in some ways you already understand them better than I. You are, after all, among those created in his image. Among those for whom he died. You are the bride of Christ. . . . You are among the privileged people. . . .
> If I look at you sometimes in apparent awe, remember it is because I know your kind and what you are capable of. . . . When you were first closed out of the Garden of God, I thought he was done with you. . . . for me, the greatest wonder is simply that you are here [in heaven] at all. (Randy Alcorn, *Deadline*, Multnomah, 101–102.)

R E F L E C T I O N

Today your students learned that they need to have a servant attitude toward others and that their motivation should come from their love for Christ. Practically, what does that mean? The next step for your students is to look for opportunities to express their love by serving people at work, at school, at home with their family, and elsewhere. Brainstorm what that will mean for each of them.

Give your students a few minutes to record honest responses to the following questions, found in their Student Notes: ***What was most meaningful to you about our experience today? What does God want you to do in response?***

Ask a student to read aloud the Summary Statements on the Student Notes.

Summary Statements

We learned today that . . .
- God commands us to be servants and have servant attitudes.
- Jesus is our model.
- If we love Jesus, we will feed and care for His sheep by being servants.

M A K E   A N   I M P A C T

. . . In Your Life
How will your students strive to be servants this week? Is there a need at the church that they can volunteer for? Are there people who need a visit? Is it just that your students need to be more conscientious on a daily basis for people that they could serve? Before they leave today, ask your students to figure out how they can be servants this week.

. . With Accountability
Have the D-Team members form pairs to become accountability partners for the week and to work on the memory verse. Have each student write out the **Unit Memory Verse,** recite it to his or her partner, and share a way the verse is meaningful in his or her life.

Prayer
Bring the students back together and close with prayer.

3. Body Language

Review

Last time, you were challenged to get involved in a part of your church to meet the need that is not being met right now in your life. How did you act on that challenge?

Focus

Within this unit you have studied what the church is and how it can meet your needs. During this experience you will be studying two instructions that Christ modeled for us while He was on earth.

THE EXPERIENCE

Instruction #1: We are to come into the body of Christ with a servant attitude.

Jesus is God of the universe and yet He came to serve not be served. List some ways Jesus was a servant while on this earth.

Instruction #2: We are to serve the body of Christ out of our love for Him.

There is another reason to be a servant to fellow believers. Read John 21:15-17.

What does this passage tell us about serving?

REFLECTION

Today you learned that you need to have a servant attitude toward others and that your motivation should come from your love for Christ.

Your next step is to look for opportunities to express your love by serving people at work, at school, at home with your family, etc. Brainstorm what that will mean for you and record your ideas in the space below.

What was most meaningful to you about our experience today?

What does God want you to do in response?

Summary Statements

We learned today that . . .
- God commands us to be servants and have servant attitudes.
- Jesus is our model.
- If we love Jesus, we will feed and care for His sheep by being servants.

MAKE AN IMPACT

. . . In Your Life
How will you strive to be a servant this week? Is there a need at the church that you can volunteer for? Are there people that need to be visited? Is it just that you need to be more conscientious on a daily basis for people that you could serve? Choose at least one action from your brainstorming list under "Reflection," and act on it this week.

. . . With Accountability
With your accountability partner, talk about your responses to the "Reflection" and "Make and Impact" questions. Exchange phone numbers. Call each other this week to hold each other accountable to making an impact in your life.

name _____ phone _____

Review your memory verse by writing it out in the space below. After reciting it to your partner, share a way the verse is meaningful in your life.

MEMORY VERSE
Ephesians 4:16

COMMUNITY

LEADER FOCUS

Community. What does it mean to you? Who models community for you? Take a close look at Christ's life. He was the Almighty God, yet He desired human companionship while on earth. What better model of community could we ask for? If you are lacking community in your life, pursue it!

BIG PICTURE

Unit Overview
In Unit 2 we will be focusing on community within the context of our D-Teams by answering three questions: (1) What is the purpose of Christian community? (2) Why should we commit to being a part of community? (3) How does God use community to change His people?

1. The Mountain
While Christian community takes many forms, during this D-Team experience your students will focus on your D-Team as a good example of Christian community. Try to help your students think of their D-Team as a mountain from which they can gain perspective on their relationship with God and others. Every D-Team member will discover that Christian community gives us two perspectives:

    1. Perspective on ourselves
    2. Perspective on others

2. Cheering Together
During this D-Team experience, your students will discover the benefits of community by looking at two Bible characters who allowed a small group of believers to surround and influence them:

    Bible Character #1: Daniel
    Bible Character #2: Jesus

3. Vital Ingredients
During this D-Team experience, your students will discover four vital ingredients necessary for life changes to take place within the context of community:

    Ingredient #1: Teaching and prayer
    Ingredient #2: Hand up and hand back

Ingredient #3: Openness and willingness to change
Ingredient #4: Full participation

Unit Memory Verse
"They devoted themselves to the apostles' teaching and to the fellowship, to the breaking of bread and to prayer" (Acts 2:42).

The Mountain

Before the D-Team Experience

LEADER DEVOTION

Suppose there were a place that you could go to that would adjust your perspective of God to 20/20 vision. Wouldn't you go there fairly often? Do you have a place like that right now? Who are the fellow Christians that help you, as a believer, gain a balanced perspective of God? How does community with other believers impact your life? As you prepare to lead, jot down your personal experiences and insights in the "Prep Notes" column so you can share them with the students.

LOOKING AHEAD

Student Focus
During this experience, your students will answer the question, *What is the purpose of Christian community?* Although Christian community takes many forms, you will focus on your D-Team, comparing your D-Team to a mountain as a safe place to gain perspective on our relationship with God and others.

Every D-Team member will discover that Christian community gives us two perspectives:

1. Perspective on ourselves
2. Perspective on others

Unit Memory Verse
"They devoted themselves to the apostles' teaching and to the fellowship, to the breaking of bread and to prayer" (Acts 2:42).

Practical Impact
Your students will be connecting the perspective you can get from being on the top of a hill to the perspective you can get from participating in a D-Team.

BE PREPARED

Materials Needed
- Bibles and pens
- Duplicated Student Notes
- Videotape, TV, VCR (Option 1)
- Binoculars for each student (Option 2)
- Recording of "The Mountain" by Steven Curtis Chapman (*Heaven in the Real World*, The Sparrow Corp., 1994)
- Tape/CD player

Special Preparation
- For Option 1: Choose a video such as *The Sound of Music, CliffHanger,* or *K-2.* Cue the videotape to a scene where people are climbing a hill or mountain.
- For Option 2: Locate a hill in your community your students can climb.

Environment
To set up the environment for this D-Team experience, you can choose one of the following. Option 1 works in any setting; Option 2 moves the experience outside your normal setting.

Option 1: If you are staying in the classroom, try to meet in a room that has several windows to access when your students are instructed to look outside the circle. Set the mood at the beginning of the D-Team experience by showing a clip of a movie with a scene of people climbing up a hill or mountain.

Option 2: The best possible place to have your D-Team experience would be on a hill that the students can climb together. It should be a place where your students can sit down in a circle and talk to each other.

Leading the D-Team Experience

(60 min. total)

GET STARTED

(5 min.)

Unit Preview
Have a student read aloud the following information under the "Preview" in the Student Notes: *As you work together through "Unit 2: Community," you will focus on community within the church by answering three questions:*
  1. **What is the purpose of Christian community?**
  2. **Why should we commit to being a part of community?**
  3. **How does God use community to change His people?**

Unit Memory Verse
Have your students read Acts 2:42, "They devoted themselves to the apostles' teaching and to the fellowship, to the breaking of bread and to prayer." Explain that the believers were devoted to learning all that Jesus Himself taught as well as participating in corporate worship, the Lord's Supper, and prayer.

Student Prayer
Ask a student to pray for God's truth to be clear to each student in your D-Team experience today.

Focus
Share with your D-Team members that this week they will answer the question, *What is the purpose of Christian community?* Explain that Christian community takes many forms, but you will focus on your D-Team as a good example of Christian community.

Tell them that during today's experience, they should think of the D-Team as a mountain from which they can gain perspective on their relationship with God and others.

Explain that every D-Team member will discover that Christian community gives us two perspectives:
  1. **Perspective on ourselves**
  2. **Perspective on others**

THE EXPERIENCE

(40 min.)

Climbing a Hill
Take your students to the bottom of a hill. Instruct them to spread at least an arm's-length apart from each other, facing the hill. Ask them to close their eyes and stand quietly for the next three minutes. Join your D-Team members in this experience, but keep track of the time. After the three minutes are over, ask your students to open their eyes and link arms to walk up the hill together. Find a place at the top of the hill to meet together.

Gather your students in a circle and discuss these questions:
  • How did you feel standing at the bottom of the hill? Alone? Afraid that everyone had left you? Unsure?
  • What did you think about?
  • How did you feel when you were able to open your eyes?

- How does sitting in this circle feel different than being at the bottom of the hill with your eyes closed?
- Which place would you rather be right now?

Perspective on ourselves

Explain to your students that today they will discover the purpose of a D-Team. Ask them to think of being part of a D-Team as like climbing a mountain. We can experience God wherever we are, but going up on a mountain allows our experience to be a safe place away from the dark valley in which we live.

Ask your students: **List the possible purposes of getting together as we do.** Their answers may include: friendships, prayer for each other, studying God's Word.

Ask your students to: **Look up the following passages to discover four essentials for building closer relationships with Christ and His body.** Have them write each essential in their Student Notes.

1. **Psalm 100:** (Worship the Lord together.)
2. **Psalm 119:9–16 and 2 Timothy 3:16:** (Study the Word together.)
3. **James 5:16:** (Prayer and accountability)
4. **Psalm 133:1 and Acts 2:42-47:** (Fellowship)

Discuss how your D-Team can build closer relationships with Christ and with one another through these four essentials.

Perspective on others

Ask: **What other perspective can we gain from being on the mountain? We have looked inward; what else can we look at from up here?**

Note that being on the mountain gives us a clearer perspective on those who are still alone down in the valley.

Ask your D-Team to stay in a circle, but turn around and face outward. Have your students leave an open space in the circle to represent an empty chair for another new person who may come up the mountain. Distribute binoculars to your students, if you have them. Ask them to describe what they can see now that they couldn't see from the bottom of the hill.

Then take a moment to remember: **How did you feel when you were at the bottom of the hill?** Alone? Unsure? No one to lean on? Emphasize that: **There are still people down there . . . alone. Who are they? Your friends? Your brother? Your sister?**

Explain that the other purpose of a D-Team is evangelism. Your students will not be able to ignore the people in the valley; they will want to bring those lonely, distraught people up to experience the mountain with them. Remind your students that they don't have to do it alone—they have their fellow D-Team members to assist them.

Read Acts 2:46-47 again. As a result of the first perspective, these people added others to their group daily. Read aloud Isaiah 12:4. What is God commanding us to do? (He tells us to worship Him, pray to Him, and tell people about Him.)

Tell them that Steven Curtis Chapman wrote a song that describes what the D-Team has talked about today. Read the words to your D-Team members and then listen to the song "The Mountain."

REFLECTION

Have your students walk down the hill together and stand alone again for three minutes. Challenge each student: ***Do you know someone who is standing in the valley alone, waiting for a guide up the mountain?*** Ask: ***What is the person's name?***

Urge students to pray for these unsaved friends. Allow your students to decide if they want to choose one person to pray for as a group, or if each wants to pray for a different friend.

Give your students a few minutes to record honest responses to the following questions, found in their Student Notes: ***What was most meaningful to you about our experience today? What does God want you to do in response?***

Ask a student to read aloud the Summary Statements in the Student Notes.

Summary Statements
We learned today that . . .
- God does not intend for anyone to be alone.
- One purpose of Christian community is to study, pray, and worship together.
- Another purpose of Christian community is evangelism: showing others how to climb the mountain.

MAKE AN IMPACT

. . . In Your Life
Ask your students to commit to praying five minutes a day for one of their friends or family members who is standing in the valley alone, waiting for a guide up the mountain.

Record the names of the people your students will be praying for, and either take the list with you each time your D-Team gets together or transfer the names to the "Prep Notes" columns of the materials you will be using. Periodically check with each D-Team member to see how the person needing prayer is doing.

. . . With Accountability
Have the D-Team members form pairs to become accountability partners for the week and to work on the memory verse. Have each student begin learning the **Unit Memory Verse** by writing it out in the space provided in the Student Notes.

Prayer
Bring the students back together and close with prayer.

1. The Mountain

Begin learning your memory verse by writing it out in the space below.

MEMORY VERSE
Acts 2:42

Preview

As you work together through "Unit 2: Community," you will focus on community within the church by answering three questions:

1. What is the purpose of Christian community?
2. Why should we commit to being a part of community?
3. How does God use community to change His people?

Unit Memory Verse

"They devoted themselves to the apostles' teaching and to the fellowship, to the breaking of bread and to prayer" (Acts 2:42).

Focus

During this experience, you will discover that Christian community gives us two perspectives: on ourselves and on others.

THE EXPERIENCE

Perspective on Ourselves

List the possible purposes of getting together as we do.

Look up the following passages to discover four essentials for building closer relationships with Christ and His body:

1. Psalm 100:

2. Psalm 119:9–16 and 2 Timothy 3:16:

3. James 5:16:

4. Psalm 133:1 and Acts 2:42–47:

Perspective on Others
What other perspective can we gain from being on the mountain?

We have looked inward; what else can we look at from up here?

How did you feel when you were at the bottom of the hill?

There are still people down there... alone. Who are they? Your friends? Your brother? Your sister?

Read Acts 2:46-47 again. As a result of the first perspective, these people added others to their group daily. Read aloud Isaiah 12:4. What is God commanding us to do?

REFLECTION

Do you know someone who is standing in the valley, waiting for you to take him or her up the mountain? What is his or her name?

What was most meaningful to you about our experience today?

What does God want you to do in response?

Summary Statements

We learned today that. . . .
- God does not intend for anyone to be alone.
- One purpose of Christian community is to study, pray, and worship together.
- Another purpose of Christian community is evangelism: showing others how to climb the mountain.

MAKE AN IMPACT

. . . In Your Life
Will you commit to praying five minutes a day for a friend who is standing in the valley alone and waiting for a guide up the mountain? Write your friend or family member's name below.

. . . With Accountability
With your accountability partner, talk about your responses to the "Reflection" and "Make an Impact" questions. Exchange phone numbers. Call each other this week to hold each other accountable to making an impact in your life.

Cheering Together

2

Before the D-Team Experience

LEADER DEVOTION

Friends fall into three categories: acquaintances, casual friends, and soul mates. Take a look at the people around you. What kinds of friends are they? Most probably fall into the first two categories. But a soul mate is someone who shares the same interests and "clicks" with you; someone who shares your faith and beliefs; someone who encourages you, challenges you, and gently but firmly points out your weak spots so you can improve.

Who fills the role of soul mate in your life? If no one fits the bill, start a quest to find someone. If you do have a soul mate, pray for, honor, and thank God for that person! As you prepare to lead, jot down your personal experiences and insights in the "Prep Notes" column so you can share them with your students.

LOOKING AHEAD

Student Focus
During this D-Team experience, your students will answer the question, *Why should we commit to being a part of community?* They will discover the benefits of community by looking at two Bible characters who allowed a small group of believers to surround and influence them:

 Bible Character #1: Daniel
 Bible Character #2: Jesus

Unit Memory Verse
"They devoted themselves to the apostles' teaching and to the fellowship, to the breaking of bread and to prayer" (Acts 2:42).

Practical Impact
During this experience, your students will cheer for the same teams and for opposing teams, and assess the support and community that comes from being on the same team.

BE PREPARED

Materials Needed
- Bibles and pens
- Duplicated Student Notes
- Video of a sports game or event, or tickets to an actual game
- TV, VCR

Special Preparation
- For Option 1: Tape a sports event between two teams who are unequal in

sports ability —OR— Collect newspaper articles about a sports event where one team was overwhelmingly defeated.

- For Option 2: Secure tickets for a local team sports event for your D-Team members.
- Read Daniel 2:1–18 to familiarize yourself with the complete story of why Daniel was before the king. Be prepared to summarize this passage for your students.

Environment

To set up the environment for this D-Team experience, you can choose one of the following. Option 1 works in any setting; Option 2 moves the experience outside your normal setting.

Option 1: Show a videotape of highlights of a sports event between two teams. If one team is overwhelmingly defeated, there will be no question for whom everyone will cheer. Or bring in a newspaper article about a similar scenario and read the highlights to your students.

Option 2: Take your D-Team members to an actual team sports event (high school level). Sit in the stands and watch for about fifteen minutes. Then go to a quieter place to finish the study.

Leading the D-Team Experience
(60 min. total)

GET STARTED

(5 min.)

Review
Have a student read aloud the following question under "Review" in the Student Notes: ***Were you able to fulfill your commitment this week to pray five minutes a day for a friend or family member?*** Check with each D-Team member to see how the person needing prayer is doing.

Student Prayer
Ask a veteran D-Team member to open in prayer.

Focus
Share with your D-Team members that this week they will answer the question, *Why should we commit to being a part of community?* They will discover the benefits of community by looking look at two Bible characters who allowed a small group of believers to surround and influence them:

Bible Character #1: Daniel
Bible Character #2: Jesus

THE EXPERIENCE

(40 min.)

Sports Event
Either attend the beginning of a sports event or watch a videotape of a sports event. Privately instruct one of your students to cheer against the majority of the crowd or other D-Team members. Allow this to go on until it causes a little bit of a stir. Then either leave the game or turn off the video. Gather your students together and discuss these questions: ***How did you feel about the student who was cheering against you? Were you upset? Did you try to convince the student to change his or her loyalty?***

Then ask the student you chose to describe how he or she felt about the students who were cheering against him or her. Was the student worn down by the opposition? Did he or she want to give in and cheer for the same team as everyone else?

Discuss with your students: ***Did you want to support the one opposing student? Why or why not?***

Read the following quote to your students.

> I'm writing this chapter on a Saturday morning in Boston. I came here to speak at a conference. After I did my part last night, I did something very spiritual: I went to a Boston Celtics basketball game. I couldn't resist. Boston Gardens is a stadium I'd wanted to see since I was a kid. Besides, Boston was playing my favorite team, the San Antonio Spurs.
>
> As I took my seat, it occurred to me that I might be the only Spurs fan in the crowd. I'd be wise to be quiet. But that was hard to do. I contained myself for a few moments, but that's all. By the end of the first quarter I was letting out solo war whoops every time the Spurs would score.

People were beginning to turn and look. Risky stuff, this voice-in-the-wilderness routine.

That's when I noticed I had a friend across the aisle. He, too, applauded the Spurs. When I clapped, he clapped. I had a partner. We buoyed each other. I felt better.

At the end of the quarter I gave him the thumbs-up. He gave it back. He was only a teenager. No matter. We were united by the higher bond of fellowship.

That's one reason for the church. All week you cheer for the visiting team. You applaud the success of the One the world opposes. You stand when everyone sits and sit when everyone stands. At some point you need support. You need to be with folks who cheer when you do. You need what the Bible calls fellowship. And you need it every week.

After all, you can only go so long before you think about joining the crowd. (Max Lucado, *When God Whispers Your Name*, Word, 145–46).

Tell your students you want to look at two Bible characters who model the need to have people around us who are "cheering for the same side."

Bible Character #1: Daniel

Have your students *quickly read Daniel 1:1–21.* Briefly explain the circumstances of Daniel's situation. Point out that Judah had been exiled to Babylonia because of disobedience. Possibly a member of Judah's royal family, Daniel was taken captive to Babylon around 605 B.C.

Ask a student to *read aloud Daniel 1:6, 11–17.* Discuss the following:

List the characters mentioned in these verses. (There were three other men with Daniel/Belteshazzar—Hananiah/Shadrach, Mishael/Meshach, and Azariah/Abednego.)

In verses 11–15, who took the test and what were the results? Why? (Daniel asked that the four young men be tested together. They relied on God and each other to get through this test. They all passed with flying colors!)

What did God give the four young men? (God gave them knowledge and understanding of all kinds.)

Briefly familiarize your students with the complete story of why Daniel was before the king. Then ask a student to *read aloud Daniel 2:12–18.* Discuss these questions:

Why did Daniel go in to the king? (Daniel and his friends' lives were on the line.)

Did Daniel know the interpretation of the dream when he went before the king? (No, Daniel did not know the interpretation of the dream—yet he went on faith that God would reveal it to him!)

What did Daniel do right after he spoke with the king? (He went home and informed his friends about the matter. Then they prayed together, and God honored what they had done.)

Bible Character #2: Jesus

Ask a student to *read aloud Matthew 4:17-22, 25.* Ask: *How did Jesus tell people about Himself and His mission on earth?* (Jesus chose to surround Himself with people who wanted to pursue the same goals as He did.)

For more insight, ask a student to **read aloud Mark 9:2–4, 9–10 and Luke 8:51**. Point out that in each passage, Jesus chose a small group of followers to share in His experiences.

Tell your students that if they were to read through the Gospels, they would find several times that the disciples and Christ come together to fellowship, learn, find refreshment, and celebrate the miraculous things that had been happening to them. There isn't a passage that tells us they became the best of friends. They were from all different walks of life and yet they had a common vision and goal—to become "fishers of men" (Matt. 4:19).

REFLECTION

 (5 min.)

Ask two students to **read aloud Ecclesiastes 4:9-12 and Matthew 18:20.** Ask: *What does it mean to not stand alone? Is there a possibility that one or more of your friends have never understood or felt the need for community in their lives?* Ask your students to share whether they want to be more committed to the D-Team. Encourage them to commit to attending the next seven D-Team experiences. Set a date when your D-Team members will be able to celebrate this accomplishment and all that they have learned. This may be a time of recommitment for some of your students.

Give your students a few minutes to record honest responses to the following questions, found in their Student Notes: *What was most meaningful to you about our experience today? What does God want you to do in response?*

Ask a student to read aloud the Summary Statements in the Student Notes.

Summary Statements

We learned today that . . .
- God never intended for us to be alone in our pursuit of Him.
- Daniel relied on his three friends to see him through difficult times.
- Even Jesus surrounded Himself with a small band of followers.

MAKE AN IMPACT

 (10 min.)

. . . In Your Life
Suggest that your students spend five to ten minutes a day journaling or praying for the other members of their D-Team. Challenge each D-Team member to give someone in the D-Team a call during the week. Encourage D-Team members to let each other know how grateful they are for one another's participation in the D-Team.

. . . With Accountability
Have the D-Team members form pairs to become accountability partners for the week and to work on the memory verse. Have each student write out the **Unit Memory Verse** and recite it to his or her partner.

Prayer
Bring the students back together and close with prayer.

2. Cheering Together

Review

Were you able to fulfill your commitment this week to pray five minutes a day for a friend or family member?

Focus

During this experience, you will answer the question, *Why should we commit to being a part of community?* You will discover the benefits of community by looking at two Bible characters who allowed a small group of believers to surround and influence them.

THE EXPERIENCE

Sports Event

How did you feel about the student who was cheering against you? Were you upset? Did you try to convince the student to change his or her loyalty?

Did you want to support the one opposing student? Why or why not?

Bible Character #1: Daniel

Quickly read Daniel 1:1–21 to get an overview of Daniel's situation. Then reread Daniel 1:6, 11–17. List the characters mentioned in these verses.

MAKE AN IMPACT

. . . In Your Life

Try spending five to ten minutes a day journaling or praying for the other people in your group. Give someone in your group a call during the week. Let the person know how grateful you are for his or her participation.

. . . With Accountability

With your accountability partner, talk about your responses to the "Reflection" and "Make an Impact" questions. Exchange phone numbers. Call each other this week to hold each other accountable to making an impact in your life.

name _____ phone _____

Review your memory verse by writing it out in the space below. Then recite it to your partner.

MEMORY VERSE
Acts 2:42

In verses 11–15, who took the test and what were the results? Why?

What did God give the four young men?

Read Daniel 2:12–18. Why did Daniel go in to the king?

Did Daniel know the interpretation of the dream when he went before the king?

What did Daniel do right after he spoke with the king?

Bible Character #2: Jesus
Read Matthew 4:17–22, 25. How did Jesus tell people about Himself and His mission on earth?

For more insight, read Mark 9:2–4, 9–10 and Luke 8:51.

R E F L E C T I O N

Read Ecclesiastes 4:9–12 and Matthew 18:20. What does it mean to not stand alone?

Is there a possibility that one or more of your friends have never understood or felt the need for community in their lives? Be prepared to share whether you want to be more committed to meeting together. Consider committing to attending the next seven student experiences. Set a date with your friends when you will be able to celebrate this accomplishment and all that you have learned. This may also be a time of recommitment.

What was most meaningful to you about our experience today?

What does God want you to do in response?

Summary Statements

We learned today that . . .
• God never intended for us to be alone in our pursuit of Him.
• Daniel relied on his three friends to see him through difficult times.
• Even Jesus surrounded Himself with a small band of followers.

Vital Ingredients

Before the D-Team Experience

LEADER DEVOTION

When you prepare to go into your D-Team, are you aware of the four ingredients of community God uses to transform us? Do you contribute and participate fully, expecting God to teach you something as well?

There are times we go through the motions and don't realize the Holy Spirit is just waiting for us to tune into His gentle voice. He wants to teach us every time we open God's Word. Are you ready to be taught something about your faith? Get ready! As you prepare to lead, jot down your personal experiences and insights in the "Prep Notes" column so you can share them with your students.

LOOKING AHEAD

Student Focus

During this D-Team experience, you will be answering the question, *How does God use community to change His people?* Every D-Team member will discover four vital ingredients necessary for life changes to take place within the context of community:

Ingredient #1: Teaching and prayer
Ingredient #2: Hand up and hand back
Ingredient #3: Openness and willingness to change
Ingredient #4: Full participation

Unit Memory Verse

"They devoted themselves to the apostles' teaching and to the fellowship, to the breaking of bread and to prayer" (Acts 2:42).

Practical Impact

Your students will be working with the ingredients of a cookie recipe during your D-Team experience and then talking about four different ingredients needed to make a good D-Team work.

BE PREPARED

Materials Needed

- Bibles and pens
- Duplicated Student Notes
- Notecards with the D-Team ingredients and verses written on them
- Ingredients for cookies
- Bowl, utensils to measure and mix the ingredients, cookie sheet
- Duplicated copies of the cookie recipe
- TV, VCR
- Cooking video (e.g., *Frugal Gourmet, The French Chef*)
- Aprons, chef bibs (Option 2)

Special Preparation

- Choose a simple cookie recipe for your students to prepare. Prior to the D-Team experience, test out your recipe to make sure it is correct.
- Prepare notecards by writing down the following information:

Recipe for Community

Ingredient #1: Teaching and prayer (Acts 2:42)
Ingredient #2: Hand up and hand back (Acts 2:44)
Ingredient #3: Openness and willingness to change (Gal. 1:23–24)
Ingredient #4: Full participation (Act 2:42)

Environment

To set up the environment for this D-Team experience, you can choose one of the following. Option 1 works in any setting; Option 2 moves the experience outside your normal setting.

Option 1: Have a cooking video playing as your students arrive. If you are unable to meet near a kitchen, bring a small toaster oven. If no cooking facilities are available, bring a sample of the finished recipe to share with your D-Team members.

Option 2: Try meeting in a kitchen or even a large cafeteria where you won't be interrupted. Provide your students with aprons or chef bibs as they work on the recipe.

Leading the D-Team Experience
(60 min. total)

GET STARTED

Review

Have a student read aloud the following information under the "Review" in the Student Notes: *Last week, you were challenged to spend five to ten minutes a day journaling or praying for your friends. You were also encouraged to give a friend a call and let that person know you were glad he or she is a part of your student experience. Did you follow through with your commitment?* Invite each student to respond.

Student Prayer

Ask a student to pray for honesty and that your students will take a collective step forward today.

Focus

Share with your D-Team members that this week they will be answering the question, *How does God use community to change His people?* Every D-Team member will discover four vital ingredients necessary for life changes to take place within the context of community:

> **Ingredient #1: Teaching and prayer**
> **Ingredient #2: Hand up and hand back**
> **Ingredient #3: Openness and willingness to change**
> **Ingredient #4: Full participation**

THE EXPERIENCE

Cookie Recipe

As your students arrive, give each student one of the ingredients for the cookie recipe you have chosen ahead of time. For example, give sugar to one student and butter to another, until all the ingredients have been distributed. Provide mixing bowls, cookie sheets, and the appropriate measuring utensils to contribute the amounts called for in the recipe. Finally, provide each student with a copy of the recipe.

Begin this D-Team experience by telling your students they are responsible for getting the correct amount of each ingredient into the recipe. Read the first ingredient and ask the student with that ingredient to put it in the mixing bowl. Continue through the recipe until all ingredients are added. Put someone in charge of the stirring when it is needed.

While the cookies are baking, take time to discuss: *What would have happened if someone didn't contribute his or her ingredient, or put in the wrong amount of it?* Ask: *What if we had just substituted one ingredient for another—would it have changed the flavor? How? Would we have been disappointed with the results? Why?*

Distribute notecards with the Recipe for Community. Read aloud the ingredients and then lead your students in a discussion of each.

Ingredient #1: Teaching and prayer (Acts 2:42)

- -

Prep Notes

Read Ingredient #1 off the notecard. Have a student **read aloud Acts 2:42**. Note that the context of this verse comes right after Pentecost when Peter preached the Gospel and about three thousand people became new believers. These new Christians united with other believers and were taught by the apostles. Emphasize that new believers in Christ need to be in a community where they can learn God's Word, pray, and mature in their faith. Ask: **Is this ingredient evident in our student "community"? Is there enough of this ingredient to make our student community "taste great"? Or do we need to add more to the mix? In other words, do you feel as though there is enough teaching of God's Word and prayer in our times together?** Discuss and ask for suggestions on what changes might need to be made.

Ingredient #2: Hand up and hand back (Acts 2:44)

Read Ingredient #2 off the notecard. Have a student **read aloud Acts 2:44**. Explain that the context of this verse is the same as that of Ingredient #1. These first Christians gathered in groups to learn and grow. That would represent the hand up—growth within their personal relationships with Jesus. Point out that verse 44 indicates that a natural result of a hand up is a hand back—reaching out to those around us and recognizing them as brothers and sisters in the family of God. Luke, the writer of the Book of Acts, states that the believers "were together and had everything in common."

Emphasize that, as members of God's family, we are responsible to help one another in every way possible. Ask: **Is this ingredient evident in our student "community"? Is there enough of this ingredient to make our student community "taste great"? Or do we need to add more to the mix? In other words, do you feel as though there is enough hand up and hand back in our times together?** Discuss and ask for suggestions on what changes might need to be made.

Ingredient #3: Openness and willingness to change (Gal. 1:23–24)

Read Ingredient #3 off the notecard. Have a student **read aloud Galatians 1:23–24**. Explain that in this passage Paul is describing his changed life. The change was so dramatic that believers in the churches of Judea could do nothing but praise God! Ask: **Are you aware of changes that are taking place within the lives of your fellow group members?**

Read Ephesians 4:29, 32. Emphasize that in order to see results on a group level, every D-Team member needs to be committed to participate in the group. Challenge your students to encourage each other's growth both within the context of D-Team experiences and outside their weekly meetings.

Ask: **Is this ingredient evident in our student "community"? Is there enough of this ingredient to make our student community "taste great"? Or do we need to add more to the mix? In other words, do you feel as though most everyone here has an openness and willingness to change?** Discuss and ask for suggestions on what changes might need to be made.

Ingredient #4: Full participation (Acts 2:42)

Read Ingredient #4 off the notecard. Have a student **read aloud Acts 2:42**. Point out that the context of this verse is the same as that of Ingredient #1. Emphasize the first three words of the verse: "They devoted themselves." The *New American Standard Exhaustive Concordance of the Bible* (Holman Bible Publishing, 1981) defines *devoted* as: "to attend constantly, endure, to be steadfast." Note that more than attendance is implied here; rather, full participation is indicated.

Ask: **Is this ingredient evident in our student "community"? Is there enough of this ingredient to make our student community "taste great"? Or do we need** *to add more to the mix? In other words, do you feel as though there is enough participation in our times together?* Discuss and ask for suggestions on what changes might need to be made.

Be gentle but direct in challenging each of your students to fully commit themselves to participation in your D-Team experiences.

R E F L E C T I O N

(5 min.) 🕐

Quickly review which ingredients need to be added to make your D-Team healthy and flavorful. Ask your students: **List the changes we decided to make at a group level to improve our times together.**

If you put the cookies in the oven when you started, take them out now and enjoy them with your D-Team! Then give your students a few minutes to record honest responses to the following questions, found in their Student Notes: **What was most meaningful to you about our experience today? What does God want you to do in response?**

Ask a student to read aloud the Summary Statements in the Student Notes.

Summary Statements

We learned today that . . .
- A student community needs a balance of different ingredients in order for it to be healthy and functional.
- These ingredients need to be added at a group level as well as at an individual level.
- Each student is responsible for his or her contribution to the student community.
- God calls us to be fully devoted to growing in our relationship with Him.

M A K E   A N   I M P A C T

(10 min.) 🕐

. . . In Your Life
Ask your students to consider what changes they need to make at an individual level to improve the student small group experiences? Instruct them to record in their Student Notes an area that they will be working on personally.

. . . With Accountability
Have the D-Team members form pairs to become accountability partners for the week and to work on the memory verse. Have each student write out the **Unit Memory Verse**, recite it to his or her partner, and share a way the verse is meaningful in his or her life.

Prayer
Bring the students back together and close with prayer.

Prep Notes

- -

Learning to Serve • Unit 2 Leader's Notes • 3. Vital Ingredients 59

3. Vital Ingredients

Review
Last week, you were challenged to spend five to ten minutes a day journaling or praying for your friends. You were also encouraged to give a friend a call and let that person know you were glad he or she is a part of your student experience. Did you follow through with your commitment?

Focus
Today, you will be answering the question, *How does God use community to change His people?* You will discover four vital ingredients necessary for life changes to take place within the context of community.

THE EXPERIENCE

Cookie Recipe
While the cookies are baking, take time to think about what would have happened if someone hadn't contributed his or her ingredient, or if someone had put in the wrong amount of an ingredient.

What if we had just substituted one ingredient for another—would it have changed the flavor? How?

Would you have been disappointed with the results? Why?

MAKE AN IMPACT

. . . In Your Life
What changes do you need to make at an individual level to improve the student small group experience? Record in the space below an area you will be working on personally.

. . . With Accountability
With your accountability partner, talk about your responses to the "Reflection" and "Make an Impact" questions. Exchange phone numbers. Call each other this week to hold each other accountable to making an impact in your life.

name   phone

Review your memory verse by writing it out in the space below. After reciting it to your partner, share a way the verse is meaningful in your life.

MEMORY VERSE
Acts 2:42

Ingredient #1: Teaching and prayer

Read Acts 2:42. Is this ingredient evident in our student community "community"? Is there enough of this ingredient to make our student community "taste great"? Or do we need to add more to the mix? In other words, do you feel as though there is enough teaching of God's Word and prayer in our times together?

Ingredient #2: Hand up and hand back

Read Acts 2:44. Is this ingredient evident in our student community "community"? Is there enough of this ingredient to make our student community "taste great"? Or do we need to add more to the mix? In other words, do you feel as though there is enough hand up and hand back in our time together?

Ingredient #3: Openness and willingness to change

Read Galatians 1:23-24. Are you aware of changes that are taking place within the lives of your fellow group members?

Is this ingredient evident in our student community "community"? Is there enough of this ingredient to make our student community "taste great"? Or do we need to add more to the mix? In other words, do you feel as though most everyone here has an openness and willingness to change?

Ingredient #4: Full participation

Read Acts 2:42. Is this ingredient evident in our student community "community"? Is there enough of this ingredient to make our student community "taste great"? Or do we need to add more to the mix? In other words, do you feel as though there is enough participation in our student community?

Page 2

REFLECTION

List the changes we decided to make at a group level to improve our times together.

What was most meaningful to you about our experience today?

What does God want you to do in response?

Summary Statements

We learned today that . . .
- A student community needs a balance of different ingredients in order for it to be healthy and functional.
- These ingredients need to be added at a group level as well as at an individual level.
- Each student is responsible for his or her contribution to the student community.
- God calls us to be fully devoted to growing in our relationship with Him.

Page 3

Unit 3 Introduction

LEADER FOCUS

"When we talk of a man doing anything for God or giving anything to God, I will tell you what it is really like. It is like a small child going to its father and saying, 'Daddy, give me six-pence to buy you a birthday present.' Of course, the father does, and he is pleased with the child's present" (C.S. Lewis, as quoted in *Draper's Book of Quotations for the Christian World* [Wheaton, IL: Tyndale, 1992], 561). If we can see that the spiritual gifts God has given us will delight Him if we just give them back, we will be motivated to pursue sharing our gifts all the more.

BIG PICTURE

Unit Overview
In Unit 3 we will be focusing on our students' spiritual gifts. They will learn about the purpose of spiritual gifts by answering three questions: (1) What are spiritual gifts and where do they come from? (2) Why do we have spiritual gifts? (3) How do I know what my spiritual gift is?

1. Birthday Gifts
During this D-Team experience, your students will examine this two-part question: *What are spiritual gifts and where do they come from?* Every D-Team member will respond to this question by discovering these three answers:

>   Answer #1: Spiritual gifts are special God-given abilities.
>   Answer #2: Spiritual gifts are given by the Holy Spirit to each believer at his or her spiritual birth.
>   Answer #3: Spiritual gifts should not be confused with natural talents or the fruit of the Spirit.

2. Body Functions
During this D-Team experience, your students will discover two reasons why we have spiritual gifts:

>   Reason #1: To enhance the spiritual growth of the body of Christ
>   Reason #2: To glorify God—not ourselves

3. Taking Inventory
During this D-Team experience, your students will begin the journey of discovering the spiritual gift that God has given to them by taking three steps:

STUDENT IMPACT

Step #1: Take a personal inventory.
Step #2: Receive peer affirmation.
Step #3: Experiment outside the student experience.

Unit Memory Verse
"There are different kinds of gifts, but the same Spirit. There are different kinds of service, but the same Lord. There are different kinds of working, but the same God works all of them in all men. Now to each one the manifestation of the Spirit is given for the common good" (1 Cor. 12:4–7).

Birthday Gifts

Before the D-Team Experience

LEADER DEVOTION

Read Matthew 25:14–30. Take a close look at what Jesus was trying to say through this parable. With what has God entrusted *you*? Material resources? Maybe your talents? Or could it be your time? Whatever God has given you to be used to glorify His name, would He come home to find you have invested it wisely? It is not too late. Invest today and bring glory, honor, and praise to Jesus! As you prepare to lead, jot down your personal experiences and insights in the "Prep Notes" column so you can share them with your students.

LOOKING AHEAD

Student Focus
During this D-Team experience, your students will examine this two-part question: *What are spiritual gifts and where do they come from?* Every D-Team member will respond to this question by discovering these three answers:

Answer #1: Spiritual gifts are special God-given abilities.
Answer #2: Spiritual gifts are given by the Holy Spirit to each believer at his or her spiritual birth.
Answer #3: Spiritual gifts should not be confused with natural talents or the fruit of the Spirit.

Unit Memory Verse
"There are different kinds of gifts, but the same Spirit. There are different kinds of service, but the same Lord. There are different kinds of working, but the same God works all of them in all men. Now to each one the manifestation of the Spirit is given for the common good" (1 Cor. 12:4–7).

Practical Impact
Your students will be using actual wrapped gifts to symbolize spiritual gifts we have been given from God.

BE PREPARED

Materials Needed
- Bibles and pens
- Duplicated Student Notes
- Flip chart, chalkboard, or dry erase board
- 23 notecards to write each spiritual gift and their definition
- 23 gift boxes all different sizes to wrap each notecard in (weight them a little with stones)
- 23 gift tags
- Birthday decorations, cake or cupcakes

Special Preparation

- Put your students' names on the gift tags. Check with your students during the week to find out if anyone new will be coming to this D-Team experience so you can put their names on gifts as well.
- Record one spiritual gift on each notecard using the following **Spiritual Gifts Reference Key**:

Spiritual Gifts Reference Key

1. Giving: The God-given ability to give money/material goods freely to the work of the Lord with happiness.
2. Hospitality: The God-given ability to care for new or needy people by providing food, shelter, and friendship.
3. Craftsmanship: The God-given ability to encourage ministry through the creative construction using tools—hands on.
4. Evangelism: The God-given ability to effectively communicate the Gospel message to seekers so they may find Christ.
5. Administration: The God-given ability to understand what makes a ministry function and then plan and carry it out.
6. Encouragement: The God-given ability to affirm and give strength to those who are discouraged and unsure of their faith.
7. Creative Communication: The God-given ability to communicate God's truth through a variety of art forms.
8. Shepherding: The God-given ability to lead, care for, and grow up others in the body of Christ.
9. Mercy: The God-given ability to cheerfully help people who are suffering.
10. Counseling: The God-given ability to effectively listen and assist someone in his or her journey to be whole as a person.
11. Teaching: The God-given ability to understand, clearly explain, and apply God's Word to people who are listening.
12. Prophecy: The God-given ability to proclaim God's truth with power, clearness, and sensitivity that will cause repentance, encouragement, and correction in people's lives.
13. Leadership: The God-given ability to attract, lead, and motivate people to accomplish the work of ministry.
14. Helps: The God-given ability to attach spiritual value to the physical tasks in the body of Christ.
15. Discernment: The God-given ability to distinguish between truth and error.
16. Faith: The God-given ability to see the Lord's will and act on it with an immovable belief in God's ability.
17. Apostleship: The God-given ability to start churches and oversee their progress.
18. Knowledge: The God-given ability to gather and analyze information effectively.
19. Healing: The God-given ability to be God's channel to restore people to health.
20. Interpretation: The God-given ability to make known to the church the message of someone speaking in tongues.
21. Tongues: The God-given ability to speak in unknown languages.
22. Miracles: The God-given ability to do powerful acts which authenticate the message of Christ and glorify God.
23. Wisdom: The God-given ability to apply knowledge effectively.

Environment

To set up the environment for this D-Team experience, you can choose one of the following. Option 1 works in any setting; Option 2 moves the experience outside your normal setting.

Option 1: Decorate your meeting room for a birthday party for your students. Serve birthday cake or cupcakes.

Option 2: Try to meet at someone's house or, if it's a nice day, meet outdoors. Wherever you gather, make it a surprise birthday party for your students.

Leading the D-Team Experience
(60 min. total)

GET STARTED

(5 min.)

Unit Preview
Have a student read aloud the information under the "Preview" in the Student Notes:
As you work together through "Unit 3: Spiritual Gifts," you will learn about the purpose of spiritual gifts by answering three questions:

1. **What are spiritual gifts and where do they come from?**
2. **Why do we have spiritual gifts?**
3. **How do I know what my spiritual gift is?**

Unit Memory Verse
Read aloud 1 Corinthians 12:4–7, "There are different kinds of gifts, but the same Spirit. There are different kinds of service, but the same Lord. There are different kinds of working, but the same God works all of them in all men. Now to each one the manifestation of the Spirit is given for the common good." Explain that these verses show the diversity and the unity of spiritual gifts.

Student Prayer
Ask a student to pray for a clear perspective on spiritual gifts today.

Focus
During this D-Team experience, your students will examine the two-part question, *What are spiritual gifts and where do they come from?* Every D-Team member will respond to this question by discovering these three answers:

Answer #1: **Spiritual gifts are special God-given abilities.**
Answer #2: **Spiritual gifts are given by the Holy Spirit to each believer at his or her spiritual birth.**
Answer #3: **Spiritual gifts should not be confused with natural talents or the fruit of the Spirit.**

THE EXPERIENCE

(40 min.)

Birthday Party
Begin this D-Team experience by telling your students you are having a birthday party for everyone in your D-Team. Emphasize that the party is not to celebrate their natural birth, but to celebrate their spiritual birth—the day that they became Christians. If you have non-Christians in your D-Team, include them in this time as well, but be sure to emphasize that we are given these spiritual gifts only at our time of salvation. Encourage those who don't have spiritual birthdays yet to listen and feel free to ask questions.

Before you distribute the gifts, serve birthday cake or cupcakes and sing a round of "Happy Birthday" just for kicks.

Explain to your students that you have a gift or two for each of them. Distribute the gifts, but instruct your students not to open them yet.

Prep Notes

Answer #1: Spiritual gifts are special God-given abilities.
Have your students *read Matthew 25:14–30*. Explain that this parable is about a master who entrusted three men with his money. Each man responded a little differently, and the master's response is recorded as well. Jesus told this story to illustrate the point that God gives us certain resources or gifts to be used wisely until Jesus returns. In verse 15, we are told that the master gave to each man according to his ability. Jesus is indicating that we receive what we can handle—that is why there are so many different gifts.

Read 1 Corinthians 7:7. Ask your students: *What will you do with your unopened gift when you take it home? Will you open it? Will you put it on a shelf? Will you wait a long time to find out what it is?* (Of course not! You will want to open it and use it!)

Answer #2: Spiritual gifts are given by the Holy Spirit to each believer at his or her spiritual birth.
Have a D-Team member *read aloud 1 Corinthians 12:11.* Ask: *According to this verse, where do spiritual gifts come from?* (From the Holy Spirit.)

Have your students *take a look at John 14:15–17.* Ask: *How is it possible for the Holy Spirit to give us spiritual gifts?* (Jesus promised that the Holy Spirit will live within us. He is the very presence of God within us. If He lives within us when we accept Jesus as our Lord, then He can give us gifts directly.)

Answer #3: Spiritual gifts should not be confused with natural talents or fruit of the Spirit.
Have your students *read 1 Corinthians 4:7.* Ask: *How would you describe the difference between spiritual gifts and natural talents?* (Spiritual gifts are given only to believers. Natural talents, on the other hand, are given to everyone at their physical birth. Natural talents are used to improve or edify ourselves, whereas spiritual gifts are used to edify the body of Christ. Natural talents include athletic ability, humor, artistic ability, etc.)

Can natural talents be transformed by a spiritual gift? (Yes. Both ought to be used under the Lordship of Jesus.)

Have your students *read Galatians 5:22–23.* Continue sharing with your students that spiritual gifts should not be confused with fruit of the Spirit. Fruit of the Spirit is a by-product of living for God. The Holy Spirit produces these character traits that are found in the nature of Christ in every Christian who desires to be more like Jesus.

Ask: *How would you describe the difference between spiritual gifts and the fruit of the Spirit?* (The significant difference is that spiritual gifts are outward, task-oriented actions that edify the body of Christ while the fruit of the Spirit results in inwardly motivated behaviors that edify the believer.)

Take a few moments to review. Ask your students to pick up one of the gifts you gave them. Tell them to picture this gift as one of the spiritual gifts you have been talking about. *Who gave you that gift?* (The gifts are God-given.) *How did you get that gift?* (The Holy Spirit gave the gift when each person became a Christian.) *Based on our definition of spiritual gifts, what do you know for sure is not in the boxes?* (There are no natural talents or fruit of the Spirit.)

Have your students open their gifts one at a time and announce the gift they have received. Make sure they understand that the gift in their box doesn't necessarily mean that God has literally given them that gift. Have a student list the name of each spiritual gift on a chalkboard or flip chart.

Prep Notes

REFLECTION *(5 min.)*

Give your students a few minutes to record honest responses to the following questions, found in their Student Notes: **What was most meaningful to you about our experience today? What does God want you to do in response?**

Ask a student to read aloud the Summary Statements in the Student Notes.

Summary Statements

We learned today that . . .
- Our spiritual gifts are God-given.
- If we are children of God, then the Holy Spirit lives in us.
- The Holy Spirit gives us our spiritual gifts.
- Spiritual gifts should not be confused with natural talents or the fruit of the Spirit.

MAKE AN IMPACT *(10 min.)*

. . . In Your Life
Challenge your students to take their gift box home and place it somewhere they will see it everyday. Ask them to commit to praying two or three minutes every time they see it, asking God to reveal to them their spiritual gift that is just waiting to be discovered. Over the next week ask your students to observe an older Christian and try to identify his or her spiritual gift. Tell your students that you will ask them the next time you get together who they observed and what spiritual gift was exercised.

. . . With Accountability
Have the D-Team members form pairs to become accountability partners for the week and to work on the memory verse. Have each student begin learning the **Unit Memory Verse** by writing it out in the space provided in the Student Notes.

Prayer
Bring the students back together and close with prayer.

1. Birthday Gifts

Preview

As you work together through "Unit 3: Spiritual Gifts," you will learn about the purpose of spiritual gifts by answering three questions:

1. What are spiritual gifts and where do they come from?
2. Why do we have spiritual gifts?
3. How do I know what my spiritual gift is?

Unit Memory Verse

"There are different kinds of gifts, but the same Spirit. There are different kinds of service, but the same Lord. There are different kinds of working, but the same God works all of them in all men. Now to each one the manifestation of the Spirit is given for the common good" (1 Cor. 12:4–7).

Focus

During this experience, you will examine this two-part question: *What are spiritual gifts and where do they come from?* You will respond to this question by discovering three answers.

THE EXPERIENCE

Birthday Party

Today we are going to celebrate your spiritual birthday—the day you asked Jesus to come into your life as Lord and Savior. That's the day you received spiritual gifts. Let's find out what that means. If you don't have a spiritual birthday yet, listen and feel free to ask questions.

Answer #1:   Spiritual gifts are special God-given abilities.

Read Matthew 25:14–30. Secondly, read 1 Corinthians 7:7. What will you do with your unopened gift when you take it home? Will you open it? Will you put it on a shelf? Will you wait a long time to find out what it is?

MAKE AN IMPACT

. . . In Your Life

Take your gift box home and place it somewhere you will see it everyday. Every time you see it pray for two or three minutes, asking God to reveal your spiritual gift to you.

During the next week, try to observe an older Christian and identify his or her spiritual gift. At our next gathering, be prepared to share who you observed and what spiritual gift was exercised.

. . . With Accountability

With your accountability partner, talk about your responses to the "Reflection" questions. Exchange phone numbers. Call each other this week to hold each other accountable to making an impact in your life.

name	phone

Begin learning your memory verse by writing it out in the space below.

MEMORY VERSE
1 Corinthians 12: 4–7

Answer #2: Spiritual gifts are given by the Holy Spirit to each believer at his or her spiritual birth.

Read aloud 1 Corinthians 12:11. According to this verse, where do spiritual gifts come from?

Read John 14:15-17. How is it possible for the Holy Spirit to give us spiritual gifts?

Answer #3: Spiritual gifts should not be confused with natural talents or the fruit of the Spirit.

Read 1 Corinthians 4:7. How would you describe the difference between spiritual gifts and natural talents?

Can natural talents be transformed by a spiritual gift?

Read Galatians 5:22-23. How would you describe the difference between spiritual gifts and the fruit of the Spirit?

Take a few moments to review. Picture the gift you received as one of the spiritual gifts we have been talking about. Who gave you that gift?

How did you get that gift?

Based on our definition of spiritual gifts, what do you know for sure is not in the boxes?

R E F L E C T I O N

What was most meaningful to you about our experience today?

What does God want you to do in response?

Summary Statements

We learned today that . . .

- Our spiritual gifts are God-given.
- If we are children of God, then the Holy Spirit lives in us.
- The Holy Spirit gives us our spiritual gifts.
- Spiritual gifts should not be confused with natural talents or the fruit of the Spirit.

Body Functions

Before the D-Team Experience

LEADER DEVOTION

Sit down and observe someone doing a task of some sort. Notice for a moment how many body parts are need to complete even the simplest task. Now take a moment to read 1 Corinthians 12:12–27. It is not surprising that God uses the body to illustrate how important spiritual gifts are to make the body of Christ function effectively. Take a few minutes to thank God for the gifts He has asked you to invest while He is away from this world. Be a good steward, so that He may say to you someday, "Well done!" As you prepare to lead, jot down your personal experiences and insights in the "Prep Notes" column so you can share them with your students.

LOOKING AHEAD

Student Focus
Every D-Team member will discover two reasons why we have spiritual gifts:

Reason #1: To enhance the spiritual growth of the body of Christ
Reason #2: To glorify God—not ourselves

Unit Memory Verse
"There are different kinds of gifts, but the same Spirit. There are different kinds of service, but the same Lord. There are different kinds of working, but the same God works all of them in all men. Now to each one the manifestation of the Spirit is given for the common good" (1 Cor. 12:4–7).

Practical Impact
Today, your students will be looking at body parts and how they need each other's spiritual gifts to make the body of Christ function smoothly—the way God designed it to work.

BE PREPARED

Materials Needed
- Bibles and pens
- Duplicated Student Notes
- Small pieces of paper with names of body parts
- Masking tape or chalk
- Strips of material or bandannas long enough to tie ankles together
- Glass of water

Special Preparation
Write the names of various body parts on small pieces of paper prior to your D-Team experience. You will want to include eyes, ears, mouth, right hand, left hand,

right foot, left foot, stomach, mind, and heart. Add additional body parts if you have more than ten students.

Environment

To set up the environment for this D-Team experience, you can choose one of the following. Option 1 works in any setting; Option 2 moves the experience outside your normal setting.

Option 1:   Clear your meeting room of any chairs, but keep one table on which to put a glass of water. Then, outline the form of a body, like one found at a murder scene, on the floor in your room with masking tape. Make it as large as possible, so that your students can spread out and sit down on different parts of it.

Option 2:   Find a setting where you can outline the form of a body on the ground with tape or chalk or rocks. Make it large enough for your students to sit on different parts of the body comfortably.

Leading the D-Team Experience
(60 min. total)

GET STARTED

(5 min.) 🕐

Review
Have a student read aloud the following information under the "Review" in the Student Notes: *Last time, you were challenged to observe an older Christian and try to identify his or her spiritual gift. Who did you observe, and what spiritual gift was exercised?* Invite each student to respond.

Student Prayer
Ask a student who shared during the review to pray for today's D-Team experience.

Focus
Share with your D-Team members that this week they will discover two reasons why we have spiritual gifts:
> **Reason #1: To enhance the spiritual growth of the body of Christ.**
> **Reason #2: To glorify God—not ourselves.**

THE EXPERIENCE

(40 min.)

Body Parts
As your students arrive, hand each person a slip of paper with the name of a body part. Inform your students that they will be role-playing their assigned body parts throughout the D-Team experience. Ask your D-Team members to sit in a circle next to the outlined body.

Begin by explaining that this D-Team experience is going to help your students discover why they need to use the spiritual gifts that God has given them. To learn this, they will be studying how our human bodies have different parts that are vital to helping it function smoothly and properly.

Ask your students to find and sit on their assigned body part. When they are situated, instruct them to think like the part they have been assigned. For example, the eye can only see—it can't give messages about hearing or smelling or picking something up. Secondly, tell your students that if the body needs to move, all the body parts can move, but they cannot lead the movement. Lastly, together they must determine if each body part is needed to complete the task. Each body part needed for the task must attach to other body parts by tying a strip of material from his or her ankle to next body part needed.

Begin the exercise by telling the **EARS** to tell the **MIND** there is a glass of water over on the table to drink. If your students need help getting started, tell the **EARS** to walk over to the **MIND** and attach themselves to each other by the **ANKLE**. Then tell them to go to the next body part they will need to carry out this command. They should work together to get to the glass of water.

If the exercise goes quickly, give them another assignment—but watch the clock! After the exercise, have your students untie their ankles, and discuss these questions: *Why did you need all these body parts to do a simple task? When asked to do*

Prep Notes

something, do you usually think about all the different parts of your body you will use to complete it? Are there any body parts represented here today you think you could do without? What are they and why?

Reason #1: To enhance the spiritual growth of the body of Christ

Ask two students to **read aloud Romans 12:4–8 and 1 Corinthians 12:12–27.** Ask: **How do these passages describe the body of Christ?** Point out these observations if they are missed:

- There are many parts to the body.
- The body of Christ is made up of many members—but one body.
- Each member belongs to the others, and each is there to help the others.
- We all have different gifts; we shouldn't withhold them from others in the body.
- We should use our spiritual gifts to help make the body complete.

Tell your students that just as the physical body parts need each other to grow, spiritual gifts are given to us and are to be used to enhance the spiritual growth of the body of Christ: our student ministry.

Reason #2: To glorify God—not ourselves

Have a student **read aloud 1 Peter 4:10–11.** Ask: **According to this passage, what is an important reason why we should use the spiritual gifts that are given to us?** (So that "in all things God may be praised through Jesus Christ.")

Have one of the students **read Matthew 5:16.** Ask: **How is God praised when we use our gifts?** (When we use them as He directs, and then the people they help will see Jesus and praise Him for the help they received.)

 (5 min.)

REFLECTION

Review with your students the two reasons why the body of Christ needs spiritual gifts. Ask your students: **Take a moment to think of a time when you saw the body of Christ work together to enhance spiritual growth and glorify God.** Invite the students to write down two to three sentences to share. Be prepared to share an observation of your own if your students are having a hard time getting started. Otherwise, let them fill this time with their experiences.

Give your students a few minutes to record honest responses to the following questions, found in their Student Notes: **What was most meaningful to you about our experience today? What does God want you to do in response?**

Ask a student to read aloud the Summary Statements in the Student Notes.

Summary Statements

We learned today that . . .

- We have spiritual gifts to enhance the body of Christ: our student ministry.
- We are to bring praise and glory to God—not ourselves—when we use our gifts.
- All of the gifts need to be used in order for the body of Christ to function smoothly and effectively.

MAKE AN IMPACT

. . . In Your Life
This next week, challenge your students to keep their eyes and hearts open to be used by God to help someone else. The way they respond may be an indication of what their gift may be and take them a step closer to discovering it. Ask them to be prepared to come to the next D-Team experience and share what happened.

. . . With Accountability
Have the D-Team members form pairs to become accountability partners for the week and to work on the memory verse. Have each student write out the **Unit Memory Verse** and recite it to his or her partner.

Prayer
Bring the students back together and close in prayer.

2. Body Functions

Review
Last time, you were challenged to observe an older Christian and try to identify his or her spiritual gift. Who did you observe, and what spiritual gift was exercised?

Focus
You will discover two reasons why we have spiritual gifts.

THE EXPERIENCE

Body Parts
As you arrive, you will be handed a slip of paper with the name of a body part. You will be studying how our human bodies have different parts that are vital to helping it function smoothly and properly. After the exercise, discuss the following questions.

Why did you need all these body parts to do a simple task?

When asked to do something, do you usually think about all the different parts of your body you will use to complete it?

MAKE AN IMPACT

... In Your Life
This next week, keep your eyes and heart open to being used by God to help someone else. The way you respond may be an indication of what your gift may be. It will take you a step closer to discovering it. Be prepared to share what happened at the next D-Team meeting.

... With Accountability
With your accountability partner, talk about your responses to the "Reflection" questions. Exchange phone numbers. Call each other this week to hold each other accountable to making an impact in your life.

name _____ phone _____

Review your memory verse by writing it out in the space below. Then recite it to your partner.

MEMORY VERSE
1 Corinthians 12: 4–7

Are there any body parts represented here today you think you could do without? What are they and why?

Reason #1: To enhance the spiritual growth of the body of Christ.
Read Romans 12:4–8 and 1 Corinthians 12:12–27. How do these passages describe the body of Christ?

Reason #2: To glorify God—not ourselves.
Read 1 Peter 4:10–11. According to this passage, what is an important reason why we should use the spiritual gifts that are given to us?

Read Matthew 5:16. How is God praised when we use our gifts?

REFLECTION

There are two reasons why the body of Christ needs spiritual gifts. One is to enhance the spiritual growth of the body of Christ. The second is to glorify God.

Take a moment to think of a time when you have seen the body of Christ work together to enhance spiritual growth and glorify God. Write yourself some notes to help you when you share.

What was most meaningful to you about our experience today?

What does God want you to do in response?

Summary Statements

We learned today that . . .
- We have spiritual gifts to enhance the body of Christ: our student ministry.
- We are to bring praise and glory to God—not ourselves— when we use our gifts.
- All of the gifts need to be used in order for the body of Christ to function smoothly and effectively.

Taking Inventory

Before the D-Team Experience

LEADER DEVOTION

Along with your students, you have been studying spiritual gifts. Perhaps you need to be challenged to reaffirm your gifts. Or maybe for the first time you are putting a name to what your heart has led you to do for the past years you have been a Christian. Stop and take the evaluations in this D-Team experience for yourself and then find someone to look over them and affirm them or maybe give you a different perspective. As you prepare to lead, jot down your personal experiences and insights in the "Prep Notes" column so you can share them with your students.

LOOKING AHEAD

Student Focus
Every D-Team member will begin the journey of discovering the spiritual gift that God has given to them by taking three steps:
   Step #1: Take a personal inventory.
   Step #2: Receive peer affirmation.
   Step #3: Experiment outside the student experience.

Unit Memory Verse
"There are different kinds of gifts, but the same Spirit. There are different kinds of service, but the same Lord. There are different kinds of working, but the same God works all of them in all men. Now to each one the manifestation of the Spirit is given for the common good" (1 Cor. 12:4–7).

Practical Impact
During this D-Team experience your students will be working through a hypothetical experience to help them begin determining what their spiritual gifts are. Then they will go through an affirmation exercise together.

BE PREPARED

Materials Needed
   • Bibles and pens
   • Duplicated Student Notes
   • Snacks and drinks (Option 1)
   • Copies of the Spiritual Gifts Reference Key (from "Unit 3, Study 1: Birthday Gifts")

Special Preparation
   Familiarize yourself with the spiritual gifts and their characteristics so that you can match them up with your students' responses during the Hypothetical Situation discussion.

Environment

To set up the environment for this D-Team experience, you can choose one of the following. Option 1 works in any setting; Option 2 moves the experience outside your normal setting.

Option 1: Since this experience results in high vulnerability, create a safe environment as much as possible. Close the door. Provide a light snack and something to drink. You may want to have music playing softly if it is not distracting.

Option 2: Try meeting at one of your student's homes. Be sure to meet in a room that can provide privacy. Include the details mentioned in Option 1.

Leading the D-Team Experience

(60 min. total)

GET STARTED

(5 min.)

Review

Have a student read aloud the following information under the "Review" on the Student Notes: *Last time you were challenged to keep your eyes and heart open to being used by God to help someone else. Be prepared to share what happened. After other students share, affirm a gift they may have used in helping that person.* Invite each student to respond.

Student Prayer

Ask a student to be prepared to pray after everyone has finished Step #1 below.

Focus

Share with your D-Team members that this week they will begin the journey of discovering the spiritual gift that God has given to them by taking three steps:

Step #1: Take a personal inventory.
Step #2: Receive peer affirmation.
Step #3: Experiment outside the student experience.

THE EXPERIENCE

(40 min.)

As your students arrive, ask them to begin taking the personal inventory in their Student Notes. Keep talking to a minimum and instruct them to think and answer for themselves.

Step #1: Take a personal inventory.
Your students will be answering the following questions in the personal inventory:

Question #1: *When I think about people in ministry, I would like to be like: (Write down names of two people—could be a student or an adult— along with two gifts you admire in those people, if they can be identified.)*

Question #2: *If it were possible for me to choose the spiritual gifts I wanted to have, I would choose these three, in this order:*

Question #3: *If I could do anything in the world I wanted to with these three gifts, I would like to . . . (This could be secular or spiritual. Also, don't let money, time, age, or education get in the way of your choices.)*

Question #4: *If you have ever been in a situation before where you have used one of those three gifts, then briefly describe the experience below.*

Emphasize to your students that this inventory is for their own personal growth, so they should answer each question as honestly and soberly as possible. In the long run, it may help them discover their spiritual gifts. Explain that there are no foolproof ways of determining spiritual gifts. Through a number of different factors, God will start to show us how He sees us personally playing a part in the body of Christ. Encourage your students to be patient. They are at a time in their lives where a lot of

---

changes take place emotionally, physically, and spiritually. This is a great time to begin evaluating and experimenting with different spiritual gifts.

After your students have completed the Personal Inventory, ask the student you selected earlier to pray for your D-Team experience.

Have your students **read 1 Timothy 4:14–15.** Ask: **What is Timothy instructing us to do in these verses, especially verse 15?** (Timothy tells us not to neglect our spiritual gifts, but to be diligent and give ourselves wholly to them by pursuing and developing them.) Explain that we will begin pursuing and developing our gifts today.

Hypothetical Situation
Explain to your students that there is a high school junior who has just lost his parents in a car accident, and you want to help him somehow. Ask them, "What can we do?" As each of your students gives a response, take notes on what they would do. Draw your quieter students into the discussion as much as possible.

Step #2: Receive peer affirmation.
Explain to your students that you would like to try to work as a team to distinguish a spiritual gift that would likely coordinate with each student's response to the high school junior just talked about.

During the next fifteen to twenty minutes, play Affirmation Hot Seat by doing two things for each student. First, affirm the student for the gift he or she displayed during the Hypothetical Situation exercise. Second, give the other students a chance to identify one gift from the Spiritual Gifts Reference Key that they see potentially being that person's spiritual gift. Encourage the student who is in the hot seat to write down all that is said about him or her.

Try to start with someone who displayed an obvious gift. For example, if a student's first response was: "I would call and let the guy know that he's important to God, and that God will take care of him" or "I would send him a care package that will help him see that I'm thinking about him and praying for him," then his gift is probably encouragement. Or, "I'd like to help him by having him stay at my house for a while" (Gift of helps). Or, "I would ask him if there is something I can give him" (Gift of giving). Continue this exercise of Affirmation Hot Seat until all students are affirmed.

 (5 min.)

REFLECTION

After completing Step #2, ask your students to take a quiet moment to compare what they wrote during Step #1: Personal Inventory, with what they wrote during Step #2: Peer Affirmation. Ask: **Was there one gift that stuck out in both steps?** Allow a moment for each student to share his or her thoughts.

Give your students a few minutes to record honest responses to the following questions, found in their Student Notes: **What was most meaningful to you about our experience today? What does God want you to do in response?**

Ask a student to read aloud the Summary Statements in the Student Notes.

Summary Statements

We learned today that . . .
    There are four ways to help discover your spiritual gift or gifts:
- personal inventory
- peer affirmation
- experimentation
- biblical/prayer affirmation

MAKE AN IMPACT

(10 min.) 🕐

. . . In Your Life

Tell your students that now that they have completed Steps #1 and #2, they have begun the journey of discovering your spiritual gifts. They are now ready for **Step #3: Experiment outside the student experience.**

Challenge your students to spend five minutes a day praying that God will give them opportunities to test and experiment with the gift or gifts that have been affirmed in them today. Close by reading 2 Timothy 1:6–7.

. . . With Accountability

Have the D-Team members form pairs to become accountability partners for the week and to work on the memory verse. Have each student write out the **Unit Memory Verse**, recite it to his or her partner, and share a way the verse is meaningful in his or her life.

Prayer

Bring the students back together and close in prayer.

---

3. Taking Inventory

Review

Last time you were challenged to keep your eyes and heart open to being used by God to help someone else. Be prepared to share what happened. After other students share, affirm a gift they may have used in helping that person.

Focus

During this experience, you will begin the journey of discovering the spiritual gift that God has given you by taking three steps.

THE EXPERIENCE

Step #1: Take a personal inventory.

This inventory is for your own personal growth, so you should answer each question as honestly and soberly as possible. You are at a time in your life where a lot of changes take place emotionally, physically, and spiritually. This is a great time to begin evaluating and experimenting with different spiritual gifts.

Question #1: When I think about people in ministry, I would like to be like: (Write down names of two people—could be a student or an adult—along with two gifts you admire in those people, if they can be identified.)

Name: _____ Gift: _____

Name: _____ Gift: _____

MAKE AN IMPACT

. . . In Your Life

Now that you have completed Steps #1 and #2, you have begun the journey of discovering your spiritual gifts. Step #3 is going to involve experimenting outside of our student experience.

Try to spend five minutes a day praying that God will give you opportunities to test and experiment with the gift or gifts that have been affirmed in you today.

. . . With Accountability

With your accountability partner, talk about your responses to the "Reflection" questions. Exchange phone numbers. Call each other this week to hold each other accountable to making an impact in your life.

_____
name   phone

Review your memory verse by writing it out in the space below. After reciting it to your partner, share a way the verse is meaningful in your life.

MEMORY VERSE
1 Corinthians 12: 4–7

Question #2: If it were possible for me to choose the spiritual gifts I wanted to have, I would choose these three, in this order:

Gift #1:

Gift #2:

Gift #3:

Question #3: If I could do anything in the world I wanted to with these three gifts, I would like to . . . (This could be secular or spiritual. Also, don't let money, time, age, or education get in the way of your choices.)

Question #4: If you have ever been in a situation before where you have used one of those three gifts, then briefly describe the experience below.

Read 1 Timothy 4:14–15. What is Timothy instructing us to do in these verses, especially verse 15?

Step #2: Receive peer affirmation.
Play Affirmation Hot Seat by doing two things for each person in the group. First, affirm the person for the gift he or she displayed during the

Hypothetical Situation exercise. Second, try to identify one gift from the Spiritual Gifts Reference Key that you see potentially being that person's spiritual gift. When it's your turn to be in the hot seat, write down all that is said about you in the space below.

R E F L E C T I O N

After completing Step #2, take a quiet moment to compare what you wrote during Step #1: Personal Inventory, with what you wrote during Step #2: Peer Affirmation. Was there one gift that stuck out in both steps?

What was most meaningful to you about our experience today?

What does God want you to do in response?

Summary Statements

We learned today that . . .
There are four ways to help discover your spiritual gift or gifts:
- personal inventory
- peer affirmation
- experimentation
- biblical/prayer affirmation

LEADER FOCUS

Our D-Teams should be service-oriented. Slow down and evaluate your own desire to serve. Are you ready? Take a heart check. When was the last time *you* did a service project for the body of Christ? In preparation for this unit, seek out an opportunity to serve. Follow the Spirit's leading.

BIG PICTURE

Unit Overview

In Unit 4 we will be focusing on our students' ownership of ministry by defining *ownership* and its implementation. Then we will follow through by planning two service opportunities. One will be within our student ministry, and the second will be within the body of Christ but outside of our student ministry. Both will take more planning and preparation than usual. Read all three experiences before committing to complete them within three weeks.

1. The Sacrifice

Ownership means giving to the body of Christ your time, talents, and treasures in response to your love for Jesus Christ. During this D-Team experience, your students will examine two questions regarding ownership:

Question #1: Why should I "own" a part of our ministry?
Question #2: How should I "own" a part of our ministry?

2. Ownership Within

During this D-Team experience, your students will practically own a part of the ministry by giving back to the body of Christ their time, talents, and treasures. They will do this by planning and following through on a service opportunity within their student ministry. Every D-Team member will take four steps to put the project into action:

Step #1: Study an example.
Step #2: Cast the vision.
Step #3: Produce a plan.
Step #4: Pray together.

3. Ownership Outside

During this D-Team experience, your students will be given an opportunity to own

STUDENT
IMPACT

their student ministry by reaching outside of it and touching lives for Christ. **NOTE: You will need to start your preparations at least one month before you actually lead this experience.** Your students will experience the value of giving through:

Gift #1: The gift we give.
Gift #2: The gift we receive.

Unit Memory Verse
"Freely you have received, freely give" (Matt. 10:8b).

Unit 1 Introduction

The Sacrifice

Before the D-Team Experience

LEADER DEVOTION

Take a moment before you dive into preparing for this D-Team experience and read 2 Corinthians 9:6–9. Then read verses 10–15. Then reread verses 12–15. Those who receive your gifts will be helped, will praise God, and will pray for you. Lastly, reread verses 6–9. Do these verses give you a different perspective on exercising your spiritual gifts? Do you feel refreshed in your desire to give cheerfully? As you prepare to lead, jot down your personal experiences and insights in the "Prep Notes" column so you can share them with your students.

LOOKING AHEAD

Student Focus

Ownership means giving to the body of Christ your time, talents, and treasures in response to your love for Jesus Christ. During this D-Team experience, your students will examine two questions regarding ownership:

    Question #1: Why should I "own" a part of our ministry?
    Question #2: How should I "own" a part of our ministry?

Unit Memory Verse

"Freely you have received, freely give" (Matt.10:8b).

Practical Impact

Your students will be using the symbolism of an altar and the sacrifice that is offered on it to help them grasp the focus of this D-Team experience.

BE PREPARED

Materials Needed
- Bibles and pens
- Duplicated Student Notes
- 3 to 5 small stones per student
- 3 notecards for each student

Environment

To set-up the environment for this D-Team experience, you can choose one of the following. Option 1 works in any setting; Option 2 moves the experience outside your normal setting.

    Option 1: Pile twenty-five or thirty small stones in your room to represent an altar. At the end of the experience, students will use the stones to build their own altars.

    Option 2: Get permission to build a small, permanent altar somewhere outside.

Prep Notes

Leading the D-Team Experience
(60 min. total)

🕐 **(5 min.)**

GET STARTED

Unit Preview
Have a student read aloud the information under the "Preview" on the Student Notes.
As you work together through "Unit 4: Ownership," you will be focusing on three questions:
1. ***What does it mean to have ownership of our student ministry?***
2. ***How can I serve the body of Christ within our student ministry?***
3. ***How can I serve the body of Christ outside our student ministry?***

Unit Memory Verse
Read aloud Matthew 10:8b, "Freely you have received, freely give," explaining that Jesus wanted His disciples to learn to be dependent on God for their provision so they could feel free to give to others.

Student Prayer
Ask a student to pray for spiritual memories to come back to everyone today.

Focus
Share with your D-Team members that ownership means giving to the body of Christ your time, talents, and treasures in response to your love for Jesus Christ. During this D-Team experience, they will examine two questions regarding ownership:

Question #1: Why should I "own" a part of our ministry?
Question #2: How should I "own" a part of our ministry?

🕐 **(40 min.)**

THE EXPERIENCE

Question #1: Why should I "own" a part of our ministry?
Tell your students that everyone has times in their lives where we can look back and recognize God's hand softening the clay of our hearts to be more like His. We make a mental altar, so to speak, as a reminder of God's movement in our lives. Add that the next twenty minutes will be spent reflecting and then sharing the experience and place that houses a personal mental altar on the campus of our ministry.

Have a student **read aloud Joshua 3:5, 11–17.** Ask your students: **How would this experience have challenged your belief in God?**

Now **read what God told Joshua to do next in 4:1–9.** Ask your students: **Why do you think God had them build this stone monument? How do you think the children responded when their parents or grandparents took them to the altar and told them its significance?**

Note that it is awesome to see how God is "parting the waters" for many people each week in all the different ministries and churches throughout the country. Then turn your students' attention to what God is doing in each of their hearts through the body of Christ!

Ask your students to take about three to five minutes to think of a time God told them to build an altar in memory of what God changed in their lives. Use the following questions to help your students recall a life-changing experience: **Has there been a specific time since you have been at [your ministry or church name] that you remember experiencing personal heart-change from God? Was it an event that your ministry or another ministry was doing? Were you watching or participating? Was there a worship and communion service that changed the course of your life? How about serving—did God use an opportunity to bring to light an area you needed to revive in your life?**

Have your students recall one life-changing experience and locate in their minds a specific location where it took place. Ask: **Where did you build a mental altar to remember? As a result of that life-changing event, what changed in your life?**

Ask one or two students to share their mental altar memories. There may be students who don't have a story or don't want to share a story. Assure them that it is okay, and encourage them to relax and celebrate with the other students.

After your students have shared their stories, explain to them that you are answering the question, *Why should I "own" a part of our ministry?* Take a moment to hand out three to five stones to each student. You may want to build one altar in the middle of your room, or you could have each student build a small, individual altar. Explain that the altar is a memorial of what God has done for us through the body of Christ.

Question #2: How should I "own" a part of our ministry?
Ask: **Why does God ask His people to build altars?** To answer these questions, have your students **read Exodus 20:22–24. What are altars to be used for?** Explain that in the Old Testament prior to Jesus' death and resurrection, a burnt offering was the only way to approach God and restore a relationship with Him. Burnt offerings and fellowship offerings were sacrificed on altars. In the New Testament, Jesus Himself was sacrificed on the altar, so to speak, for our sins and to restore our relationship with God. A fellowship offering (Lev. 3) was offered as an expression of gratitude to God.

Tell your students that the altar we made today is a memorial of what God has done in our lives. Ask: **What kind of fellowship offering could you give as an expression of your gratitude to God? How could you own a part of our ministry?**

Have your students **read Psalm 40:6–8.** Ask: **According to this passage, what does God desire from us?** Note that God desires for us to do His will. He covets our time. The first of our fellowship sacrifices could be our time. God wants us to follow Him, and He will give us all that we need.

Share that a second fellowship sacrifice we could offer God is our talents. Ask one of your students to **read aloud Romans 12:1, 4–6.** Ask: **According to this passage, what does God desire from us?** Explain that God desires that we offer our bodies as living sacrifices, using our gifts to please God.

Have a student read aloud **2 Corinthians 9:6–15.** Ask: **According to this passage, what does God desire from us?** Note that the third fellowship sacrifice we can offer is our treasures. Emphasize that Paul is referring to spiritual rewards.

REFLECTION

(5 min.)

Ask: **Why should we give our time, talents, and treasures to the body of Christ?** (Because it is an expression of our love for Jesus and what He has done in our lives through this ministry.)

Refer your students to the altar they built. Ask your students if they would like to make a symbolic fellowship offering to God on that altar. Distribute notecards so they can write a promise to God regarding one, two, or all of the suggested offerings: time, talents and treasures. Give them a moment to respond silently by putting their cards on top of the altar.

Give your students a few minutes to record honest responses to the following questions, found in their Student Notes: **What was most meaningful to you about our experience today? What does God want you to do in response?**

Ask a student to read aloud the Summary Statements in the Student Notes.

Summary Statements

We learned today that . . .
- We should never forget the life-change that Jesus creates in us.
- We can give back to God in gratitude for the sacrifice Jesus made for us.
- We should use our time, talents, and resources to help others experience the same life-change.

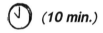 *(10 min.)*

MAKE AN IMPACT

. . . In Your Life
Ask your students what, practically speaking, does the commitment they just made look like? What will they change about their time as a result of their commitment? What will they do differently with their talents as a result of their commitment? And what will they do differently with their treasures? Ask them whether they are tithing regularly, and if they would like to start.

These steps are personal and cannot be predetermined by anyone but the student. Celebrate any changes that are determined—no matter how small they may appear to you. During the next week, encourage your students to implement the changes they have mentioned.

. . . With Accountability
Have the D-Team members form pairs to become accountability partners for the week and to work on the memory verse. Have each student begin learning the **Unit Memory Verse** by writing it out in the space provided in the Student Notes.

Prayer
Bring the students back together and close with prayer.

4. The Sacrifice

Preview

As you work together through "Unit 4: Ownership," you will be focusing on three questions:

1. What does it mean to have ownership of our student ministry?
2. How can I serve the body of Christ within our student ministry?
3. How can I serve the body of Christ outside our student ministry?

Unit Memory Verse

"Freely you have received, freely give" (Matt. 10:8b).

Focus

Today, you will examine two questions regarding ownership.

THE EXPERIENCE

Question #1: Why should I "own" a part of our ministry?

Read Joshua 3:5, 11–17. How would this experience have challenged your belief in God?

Read Joshua 4:1–9. Why do you think God had them build this stone monument? How do you think the children responded when their parents or grandparents took them to the altar and told them its significance?

Summary Statements

We learned today that . . .
- We should never forget the life-change Jesus creates in us.
- We can give back to God in gratitude for the sacrifice Jesus made for us.
- We should use our time, talents, and resources to help others experience the same life-change.

MAKE AN IMPACT

. . . In Your Life

Practically speaking, what does the commitment you just made look like? What will you change about your time as a result of your commitment? What will you do differently with your talents as a result of your commitment? Lastly, what will you do differently with your treasures? Are you tithing regularly—or ever? Would you like to start?

During the next week, try to implement the changes you have mentioned.

. . . With Accountability

With your accountability partner, talk about your responses to the "Reflection" questions. Exchange phone numbers. Call each other this week to hold each other accountable to making an impact in your life.

name _____ phone _____

Begin learning your memory verse by writing it out in the space below.

MEMORY VERSE
Matthew 10:8b

Has there been a specific time since you have been at your student ministry or church that you remember experiencing personal heart-change from God? Was it an event your ministry or another ministry was doing? Were you watching or participating? Was there a worship and communion service that changed the course of your life? How about serving—did God use an opportunity to bring to light an area you needed to revive in your life?

Recall one life-changing experience and locate in your mind a specific location that it took place. Where did you build a mental altar to remember? As a result of that life-changing event, what changed in your life? Be prepared to share your mental altar memories. If you don't have a story or don't want to share a story, relax and celebrate with the other students.

Question #2: How should I "own" a part of our ministry?
Read Exodus 20:22-24. Why does God ask people to build altars? What are altars to be used for?

The altar you made today is as a memorial of what God has done in your life. What kind of fellowship offering could you give as an expression of your gratitude to God? How could you own a part of our ministry?

Read Psalm 40:6-8. According to this passage, what does God desire from us?

Read Romans 12:1, 4-6. According to this passage, what does God desire from us?

Read 2 Corinthians 9:6-15. According to this passage, what does God desire from us?

REFLECTION

Why should we give our time, talents, and treasures to the body of Christ?

Remember the altar you built earlier? Would you like to make a symbolic fellowship offering to God on that altar? When the notecards are distributed, write a promise to God regarding one, two, or all of the suggested offerings: time, talents, and treasures. When you are ready, put your cards on top of the altar.

What was most meaningful to you about our experience today?

What does God want you to do in response?

Ownership Within

Before the D-Team Experience

LEADER DEVOTION

God wants to do miraculous things through us. We need to be willing to give Him the freedom to talk to us about accomplishing His goals. Nehemiah's life provides many principles for us to live by as leaders. First, Nehemiah kept on track with God's purpose and plan. Second, he told the people exactly what the goal was and how to get it done. Third, he lived above reproach. All the accusations about him were false. Last, Nehemiah constantly consulted his Heavenly Father for power and wisdom. In evaluating yourself, is there something you could learn from Nehemiah and then change in your life? As you prepare to lead, jot down your personal experiences and insights in the "Prep Notes" column so you can share them with your students.

LOOKING AHEAD

Student Focus

During this D-Team experience, your students will practically own a part of the ministry by giving back to the body of Christ their time, talents, and treasures. They will do this by planning and following through on a service opportunity within their student ministry. Every D-Team member will take four steps to put the project into action:

Step #1: Study an example.
Step #2: Cast the vision.
Step #3: Produce a plan.
Step #4: Pray together.

Unit Memory Verse

"Freely you have received, freely give" (Matt. 10:8b).

Practical Impact

Your students will be studying Nehemiah and the rebuilding of the wall in Jerusalem. They will relate to the citizens of Jerusalem who contributed time, money, and talents—whatever was needed—to get the job done. Your students will leave today with bricks to remind them of their responsibility.

BE PREPARED

Materials Needed
- Bibles and pens
- Duplicated Student Notes
- A brick for each student
- Permanent markers
- Student ministry logo or banner, construction tools (Option 1)
- Tools and tool belts (Option 2)

Special Preparation

- Prior to this week's D-Team experience, read Nehemiah 1:1–11. Be prepared to share with your students the historical circumstances surrounding the Book of Nehemiah.
- Before getting together with your students, spend some time in prayer. Ask God to show you what part of the "wall" in your ministry needs to be rebuilt (See Step #2). Go to your pastor or the person who holds you accountable and explain what you will be doing in this experience. Ask the person if he or she has any reservations, concerns, or ideas about this opportunity. You will want their emotional and prayer support.

Environment

To set up the environment for this D-Team experience, you can choose one of the following. Option 1 works in any setting; Option 2 moves the experience outside your normal setting.

Option 1: Your students need to be visionaries. Fill the meeting area with items that will make them proud and excited to be a part of the ministry God has given them within your church. If you have a student ministry logo or banner, display it. Display construction tools around the room for atmosphere.

Option 2: Try getting together by a large wall made of stone, brick, or cement. If possible, provide tools and tool belts for your students.

Leading the D-Team Experience
(60 min. total)

GET STARTED

Review
Have a student read aloud the following under the "Review" in the Student Notes:
Last time, you were challenged to make a change in the way that you give your time, talent, and treasure/money back to the body of Christ. Share any changes you made this past week. Invite each student to respond.

Student Prayer
Ask one of your student leaders to pray that God will be honored today.

Focus
Share with your D-Team members that during this D-Team experience, they will practically own a part of the ministry by giving back to the body of Christ their time, talents, and treasures. They will do this by planning and following through on a service opportunity within their student ministry. Every D-Team member will take four steps to put the project into action:

Step #1: Study an example.
Step #2: Cast the vision.
Step #3: Produce a plan.
Step #4: Pray together.

THE EXPERIENCE

Begin your D-Team experience by giving a brick to each of your students. Ask them to keep the bricks in front of them throughout this experience as a visual aid.

Step #1: Study an example.
Have your students ***read Nehemiah 2:1–6.*** Ask: ***What did Nehemiah want to give back to God? How did he own part of the ministry?*** (He wanted to return and rebuild the wall around the city of Jerusalem.)

Have your students ***read Nehemiah 2:11-18*** and discuss the following questions: ***What did Nehemiah do first?*** (He surveyed the damage.) ***What was Nehemiah's second step in verse 17?*** (He cast a vision.) ***How did the people respond in verse 18?*** (They were enthusiastic about rebuilding!)

Tell your students that there is a need for us to survey our ministry's wall, so to speak. Ask them whether we could use some rebuilding. For example, could the facility you meet in use some work? Maybe your budget is low and you could use some building back up.

Now, have your students ***read Nehemiah 3:1–6, 13–15, 17, 22.*** (Give one verse to each student to read.) Ask: ***What do you notice about the builders in these verses?*** (Everyone had a part to contribute. Point out that the verses in-between list people who repaired all the in-between parts of the wall.)

Prep Notes

Read Nehemiah 4:6. Ask: **How did the people work?** (With all their hearts!)

Ask a student to **read aloud Nehemiah 6:15–16.** Ask: **How quickly was the wall rebuilt?** (Fifty-two days! Amazing!) **In verse 16, how were the people able to complete the wall?** (With the help of God.) **What can we learn from this story?**

Step #2: Cast the vision.
Refer your students to your earlier question about whether your ministry could use some rebuilding. Take a moment now to explain what part of the wall they will be rebuilding. Explore some of the following opportunities or think of your own:
* Physically remodel the room in which you meet.
* Raise money for your student ministry budget through a car wash, bake sale, or cleaning houses or yards. Take pledges by the hour to do some type of community service—clean a park, pick up trash along roads, paint park buildings, etc.
* Make a banner with your student ministry's name on it.
* Make flyers/letters about your student ministry to hand out at school.

Step #3: Produce a plan.
Refer your students to the verses in Nehemiah 3 that talked about each of the workers having their parts to contribute in order to accomplish the goal. Encourage your D-Team members to fully participate in the project they have envisioned.

Step #3 can be done one of two ways. You can open up discussion and produce a plan for accomplishing the vision of rebuilding, or you can instruct your students in what needs to be done and then assign responsibilities. Appoint a student to be a record keeper of what is discussed so you can type it out later and give the plan to your students. Some questions you'll want to discuss are:
* When will the rebuilding take place?
* What materials will we need?
* Who will bring the materials?
* Which assignment will each of us have?
* What are our goals and deadlines?

After you and your students have produced a plan, ask each student to write on his or her brick the specific task that he or she will be responsible for in order for the project to get done.

Step #4: Pray together.
Tell your students that if we were to read Nehemiah 1–6, we would see that Nehemiah was a man of prayer. He prayed for God's help. He talked to Him about every step that was taken. Explain that without God involved, not only will their plan be unsuccessful; it will be done with the wrong motives.

Have your students build a wall with their bricks. Have them encircle it and pray for every aspect of the rebuilding—for each other, for protection, for God's blessing, for the glory and the praise to be directed toward God and not themselves.

 (5 min.)

REFLECTION

Your students have worked through the four steps for owning a part of their student ministry. The next step for them is to determine what their personal responsibility will involve and how they will accomplish it. Tell them: **Take a few minutes to think that through and ask any questions you might have.**

Give your students a few minutes to record honest responses to the following questions, found in their Student Notes: **What was most meaningful to you about our experience today? What does God want you to do in response?**

Ask a student to read aloud the Summary Statements in the Student Notes.

Summary Statements

We learned today that . . .
- Nehemiah was a great example of what God can do if we want to give Him our time, talents, and treasures.
- Prayer needs to play a huge part in accomplishing God's plan.
- Like Nehemiah, we need to be open to what God has planned for our lives.

MAKE AN IMPACT

(10 min.)

. . . In Your Life
Challenge your students to think through their assigned responsibilities. Ask them to consider whether their assignments require a giving of time, talent, or treasure or money? Are they able to give more than they have given so far? Remember that each student has to determine this for themselves in the quietness of their heart. Ask them to be specific about what they will do this next week that will include giving of one of these things?

. . . With Accountability
Have the D-Team members form pairs to become accountability partners for the week and to work on the memory verse. Have each student write out the **Unit Memory Verse** and recite it to his or her partner.

Prayer
Bring the students back together and close in prayer.

2. Ownership Within

Review

Last time, you were challenged to make a change in the way that you give your time, talent, and treasure or money back to the body of Christ. Share any changes you made this past week.

Focus

During this experience, you will demonstrate ownership of part of the ministry by giving back to the body of Christ your time, talents, and treasures. You will do this by planning and following through on a service opportunity within our student ministry. You will take four steps to put the project into action.

THE EXPERIENCE

Step #1: Study an example.

Read Nehemiah 2:1–6. What did Nehemiah want to give back to God? How did he own part of the ministry?

Read Nehemiah 2:11–18. What did Nehemiah do first?

What was Nehemiah's second step in verse 17?

How did the people respond in verse 18?

MAKE AN IMPACT

. . . In Your Life

Think through your assigned responsibilities. Does your assignment require a giving of time, talent, or treasure/money? Are you able to give more than you have given so far? Only you can determine that for yourself in the quietness of your heart. What specifically will you be do this next week that will include giving of one of these things?

. . . With Accountability

With your accountability partner, talk about your responses to the "Reflection" questions. Exchange phone numbers. Call each other this week to hold each other accountable to making an impact in your life.

name   phone

Review your memory verse by writing it out in the space below. Then recite it to your partner.

MEMORY VERSE
Matthew 10:8b

Read Nehemiah 3:1–6, 13–15, 17, 22. What do you notice about the builders in these verses?

Read Nehemiah 4:6. How did the people work?

Read Nehemiah 6:15–16. How quickly was the wall rebuilt?

What can we learn from this story?

In verse 16, how were the people able to complete the wall?

Step #2: Cast the vision.
Take a moment to explore what part of the wall you will be rebuilding. Your leader will be explaining what the vision will be for rebuilding the walls of your student ministry. Take notes below.

Step #3: Produce a plan.
Refer to the verses in Nehemiah 3 that talked about each of the workers having their parts to contribute in order to accomplish the goal. Take notes below on your plan.

After you have produced a plan, write on your brick the specific task that you will be responsible for in order for the project to get done.

Step #4: Pray together.
With your fellow students, build a wall with your bricks. Encircle it and pray for every aspect of the rebuilding—for each other, for protection, for God's blessing, for the glory and the praise to be directed toward God and not yourselves.

R E F L E C T I O N

You have worked through the four steps for owning a part of your student ministry. The next step for you is to determine what your personal responsibility will involve and how you will accomplish it. Take a few minutes to think through and ask any questions you might have.

What was most meaningful to you about our experience today?

What does God want you to do in response?

Summary Statements

We learned today that . . .
- Nehemiah was a great example of what God can do if we want to give Him our time, talents, and treasures.
- Prayer needs to play a huge part in accomplishing God's plan.
- Like Nehemiah, we need to be open to what God has planned for our lives.

Ownership Outside

Before the D-Team Experience

LEADER DEVOTION

Have you given anything to anyone recently? If not, put this guide down and take the time to do that right now. Don't expect anything in return or give out of obligation. If you have to, wait until your heart catches up with your head. How do you feel after doing this little assignment? What emotions did you experience? Would you do the assignment again based on how you felt? What were your motivations? Did you find it more blessed to give than to receive? Try not to forget what it was like to give a gift to someone. As you prepare to lead, jot down your personal experiences and insights in the "Prep Notes" column so you can share them with your students.

LOOKING AHEAD

Student Focus

During this D-Team experience, your students will be given an opportunity to own their student ministry by reaching outside of it and touching lives for Christ. Two gifts will be exchanged during this D-Team experience that will teach your students the values of giving:

Gift #1: The gift we give.
Gift #2: The gift we receive.

Unit Memory Verse

"Freely you have received, freely give" (Matt. 10:8b).

Practical Impact

This D-Team experience focuses on giving gifts rather than receiving gifts. It would work well at Christmas, but you can do it any time of the year.

BE PREPARED

Materials Needed

- Bibles and pens
- Duplicated Student Notes
- Tape and scissors
- Wrapping paper, bows, and gift tags

Special Preparation

- Start your preparations at least one month prior to actually having the D-Team experience. During this D-Team experience, your students will have the privilege of giving to a family who is in need by providing them with gifts and food they would be unable to purchase otherwise.
- Locate a family in need of some provisions. It could be a family with small

children, an elderly couple, or a single parent who is just trying to make ends meet. Be careful about serving a family that has a student in your ministry—you don't want to embarrass or humiliate them in front of their peers.

- Meet with your selected family and let them know what your student ministry would like to do for them. Ask the family if they would mind if your students came over for a few minutes to deliver their gifts. Set a date and time that will be convenient. Be prepared for the family to say that they would rather not have *all* the students coming to their home.
- Send a letter to your students two weeks prior to this D-Team experience. Inform them that they will be buying and then giving gifts to a family within the body of Christ. Ask them to start saving some money they can use to shop for the family. Challenge them to do some baby-sitting or extra work around the house for a little extra cash. If cash isn't an option, suggest that they bring home-baked cookies or some of their old toys or stuffed animals (that are in great condition!). Close the letter by encouraging your students to come with a giving heart. If you only have a couple of D-Team members, team up with another ministry to do this project.

Environment

To set up the environment for this D-Team experience, you can choose one of the following. Option 1 works in any setting; Option 2 moves the experience outside your normal setting.

Option 1:   Create a giving atmosphere by having a few gifts already wrapped and set out on a table. Display all the materials to wrap gifts. This will help them get the idea that they will be giving gifts to someone else.

Option 2:   Have your students meet at a mall or shopping center. Suggest that your students shop for their families prior to the D-Team study. If this setting is too distracting, then try to meet at someone's home after shopping.

Leading the D-Team Experience
(60 min. total)

GET STARTED

Review

Have a student read aloud the following question under the "Review" in the Student Notes: *Last time, you were challenged to think through the responsibility you took on regarding owning a part of your student ministry. What specifically did you do this past week that involved giving of your time, your talents, or your treasures or money?* Invite each student to respond.

Student Prayer

Begin this D-Team experience by asking your students to form a circle and then face outward and grab a hand next to them. Ask a student to pray for what will take place over the next hour.

Focus

Share with your D-Team members that during this D-Team experience, they will be given an opportunity to own their student ministry by reaching outside of it and touching lives for Christ. Two gifts will be exchanged during this D-Team experience that will teach them the values of giving:

> **Gift #1: The gift we give.**
> **Gift #2: The gift we receive.**

THE EXPERIENCE

Gift #1: The gift we give.

Ask your students to **turn to 2 Corinthians 8:2–5.** Have one of your students read it aloud. Ask: *What did these impoverished people do that impressed Paul?* (They gave as much as they were able and then some.) *Did Paul make them do it?* (No, they gave entirely on their own.)

Read aloud 2 Corinthians 8:6–9. Ask: *How do these verses relate to the first five verses?* Ask your students to recall the altars they built that represented what God has done for them. Note that the Corinthians gave out of their love and dedication to Christ as well as their love for fellow believers. Explain in detail that during this D-Team experience your students have the privilege of giving to a family who is in need by providing them with gifts and food. Answer any questions your students might have.

Gift #2: The gift we receive.

Ask: *What do you expect to get out of this whole experience? Do you expect recognition? What if we never hear from the family again, how will that affect you? Do you want to be given something in return for your generosity?*

Have your students recall giving gifts at Christmas time or a birthday. Ask: *What do you remember feeling after you gave a gift? Excitement? Unexplainable joy? A "let's do that again!" feeling?* Let your students share some memories of their own.

Explain to your students that the gift they will receive is not something tangible. It won't be something they can carry home and put in their room. But they will take it home in their hearts.

Read aloud Acts 20:35. Ask: ***What did Paul mean?*** If it is hard for your students to understand what Paul meant, let them know that they will have a much better understanding after they give their gifts to the family.

The next step for your students could be a couple of different things. If they brought unwrapped gifts, spend some time wrapping and labeling gifts. If your students haven't purchased their gifts, spend the next hour shopping together and then meet at someone's house to finish wrapping the gifts. Or if you were not able to prepare ahead of time, pick a day you can all get together and wrap gifts. Make sure your students know what day they will be delivering the gifts.

Give each student a responsibility. For example, assign a member of the family to each student. Or assign your students items such as nonperishable food items, cookies, or gift certificates. Your students will need to decide whether to pool their money and how their money will be spent.

Ask each student to write down: ***What will your responsibility be in the giving of the gifts?***

🕐 *(5 min.)*

R E F L E C T I O N

Give your students a few minutes to record honest responses to the following questions, found in their Student Notes: ***What was most meaningful to you about our experience today? What does God want you to do in response?***

Ask a student to read aloud the Summary Statements in the Student Notes.

Summary Statements

We learned today that . . .
- God has given to us freely, therefore we should give freely.
- The gift we give is out of our love for Jesus Christ.
- We shouldn't expect anything in return.
- The gift we receive for giving is an unexplainable joy in our hearts.

🕐 *(10 min.)*

M A K E A N I M P A C T

. . . In Your Life
Challenge your students to examine their lives to see if there are opportunities to give that they are overlooking. Perhaps they have an opportunity to give to their family or one of their fellow D-Team members. Ask them what part of their time, talents, or treasures could they give up for one of these people in their lives. Ask them to decide what they will do differently before they leave today.

. . . With Accountability
Have the D-Team members form pairs to become accountability partners for the week and to work on the memory verse. Have each student write out the **Unit Memory Verse**, recite it to his or her partner, and share a way the verse is meaningful in his or her life.

Prayer
Bring the students back together and close with prayer.

3. Ownership Outside

Review
Last time, you were challenged to think through the responsibility that you took on regarding owning a part of your student ministry. What specifically did you do this past week that involved giving of your time, your talents, or your treasures or money?

Focus
During this experience, you will be given an opportunity to own your student ministry by reaching outside of it and touching lives for Christ. Two gifts will be exchanged during this experience that will teach you the values of giving.

THE EXPERIENCE

Gift #1: The gift we give.
Read 2 Corinthians 8:2–5. What did these impoverished people do that impressed Paul?

Did Paul make them do it?

Read 2 Corinthians 8:6–9. How do these verses relate to the first five verses?

. . . With Accountability
With your accountability partner, talk about your responses to the "Reflection" and "Make an Impact" questions. Exchange phone numbers. Call each other this week to hold each other accountable to making an impact in your life.

name   phone

Review your memory verse by writing it out in the space below. After reciting it to your partner, share a way the verse is meaningful in your life.

MEMORY VERSE
Matthew 10:8b

Gift #2: The gift we receive.
What do you expect to get out of this whole experience? Do you expect recognition?

What if we never hear from the family again, how will that affect you? Do you want to be given something in return for your generosity?

Do you recall giving gifts at Christmas time or a birthday? What do you remember feeling after you gave a gift? Excitement? Unexplainable joy? A "let's do that again!" feeling? Share some memories of your own.

Read Acts 20:35. What did Paul mean?

If you brought unwrapped gifts, spend some time wrapping and labeling gifts. If you haven't purchased your gifts, spend the next hour shopping and then meet at someone's house to finish wrapping the gifts. Or if you were not able to prepare ahead of time, pick a day that you can all get together and wrap gifts.

What will your responsibility be in the giving of the gifts?

R E F L E C T I O N

What was most meaningful to you about our experience today?

What does God want you to do in response?

Summary Statements

We learned today that . . .
- God has given to us freely, therefore we should give freely.
- The gift we give is out of our love for Jesus Christ.
- We shouldn't expect anything in return.
- The gift we receive for giving is an unexplainable joy in our hearts.

M A K E   A N   I M P A C T

. . . In Your Life
Take some time to examine your life to see if there are opportunities to give you might be overlooking. Perhaps you have an opportunity to give to your family or one of your fellow students.

What part of your time, talents, or treasures could you give up for one of these people in your life?

Decide what you will do differently before you leave today.

Shepherding Summary Form

Complete this form immediately after every meeting and give a copy to your ministry director or small groups coordinator.

ATTENDANCE

Leader:

Apprentice leader:

Members present: Guests filling the "empty chair":

Members absent:

Starting core number:

ACTIVITY SUMMARY
Briefly describe how you incorporated the CLEAR values listed below.

Christ—How was Christ made the central focus of your time together?

Listen— Were you able to meet the students' needs to be heard? What concerns arose?

Empty chair—Are students praying for specific friends they could invite to join the small group? How are you fostering an openness to new members?

Affirm—In what ways were you able to affirm your students?

Read and pray—How effective was your time in the Word and in prayer together?

CELEBRATION
What's happening in your small group that you'd like to celebrate or note? What problems or questions do you need help with?

WILLOW CREEK

RESOURCES

This resource was created to serve you.

It is just one of many ministry tools that are part of the Willow Creek Resources® line, published by the Willow Creek Association together with Zondervan Publishing House. The Willow Creek Association was created in 1992 to serve a rapidly growing number of churches from all across the denominational spectrum that are committed to helping unchurched people become fully devoted followers of Christ. There are now more than 2,500 WCA member churches worldwide.

The Willow Creek Association links like-minded leaders with each other and with strategic vision, information, and resources in order to build prevailing churches. Here are some of the ways it does that:

- **Church Leadership Conferences**—3 1/2 -day events, held at Willow Creek Community Church in South Barrington, IL, that are being used by God to help church leaders find new and innovative ways to build prevailing churches that reach unchurched people.

- **The Leadership Summit**—a once-a-year event designed to increase the leadership effectiveness of pastors, ministry staff, volunteer church leaders, and Christians in business.

- **Willow Creek Resources®**—to provide churches with a trusted channel of ministry resources in areas of leadership, evangelism, spiritual gifts, small groups, drama, contemporary music, and more. For more information, call Willow Creek Resources® at 800/876-7335. Outside the US call 610/532-1249.

- *WCA News*—a bimonthly newsletter to inform you of the latest trends, resources, and information on WCA events from around the world.

- *The Exchange*—our classified ads publication to assist churches in recruiting key staff for ministry positions.

- **The Church Associates Directory**—to keep you in touch with other WCA member churches around the world.

- *WillowNet*—an Internet service that provides access to hundreds of Willow Creek messages, drama scripts, songs, videos and multimedia suggestions. The system allows users to sort through these elements and download them for a fee.

- *Defining Moments*—a monthly audio journal for church leaders, in which Lee Strobel asks Bill Hybels and other Christian leaders probing questions to help you discover biblical principles and transferable strategies to help maximize your church's potential.

For conference and membership information please write or call:

Willow Creek Association
P.O. Box 3188
Barrington, IL 60011-3188
ph: (847) 765-0070
fax: (847) 765-5046
www.willowcreek.org

0597